American Headway 3A

THE WORLD'S MOST TRUSTED ENGLISH COURSE

SECOND EDITION

Liz and John Soars

OXFORD UNIVERSITY PRESS

Scope and Sequence

LANGUAGE INPUT

UNIT	GRAMMAR	VOCABULARY	EVERYDAY ENGLISH
1 A world of difference *page 2*	**Naming tenses** Present, Past, Present Perfect **Auxiliary verbs** *do, be, have* p. 2 **Questions and negatives** *Where were you born? He doesn't live in Montreal.* p. 2 **Short answers** *Yes, I have. No, he didn't.* p. 4 **Spoken English – sounding polite** *"Did you have a good day?" "Yes, I did. I went shopping."* p. 4	**What's in a word?** Parts of speech and meaning *verb, adjective, noun, or adverb?* Spelling and pronunciation *vowel sounds* Word formation *active, actor, action* Words that go together *fall in love* Keeping vocabulary records p. 9	**Everyday situations** *I need to make an appointment. A medium latte, please. For here or to go?* p. 9
2 The work week *page 10*	**Present tenses** Simple and continuous *What does she do? What's she doing?* p. 10 State verbs *like, know, understand* p. 11 Passive *People are employed ... I'm being served.* p. 13 **How often ...?** *hardly ever twice a year* p. 11	**Positive and negative adjectives** *hardworking bad-tempered* p. 15 **Free time activities** *go for a run staying fit a recipe, to chop* p. 16	**Making small talk** *It's such a great city, isn't it? I was born in ..., but I live in ... Oh, good. Really? Have you? Who do you work for?* **Spoken English – softening a negative comment** *a bit late not very big* p. 17
3 Good times, bad times *page 18*	**Past tenses** Simple and continuous *He worked in London. He was studying art.* p. 19 **Past Perfect** *He had fallen in love. He'd been arguing.* p. 19 **used to** *He used to wake up at 6:00.* p. 19	**Spelling and pronunciation** *good /gʊd/, food /fuːd/ male, mail* /u/ *tooth truth juice* p. 21 **Lost sounds** *chocolate foreign* p. 21	**Giving opinions** *He's really great, isn't he? Definitely! Mmm! That's not true!* **Spoken English – making an opinion stronger** *just awful absolutely adore* p. 25
4 Getting it right *page 26*	**Advice, obligation, and permission** Modal and related verbs *You should check online. You must tell your neighbors. They can get married at 18. You are allowed to go. Children had to go to school. They didn't have to work.* pp. 26–28	**Phrasal verbs (1)** Literal or idiomatic? *She took her boots off. His business has taken off. The flight took off on time.* Separable or inseparable? *He turned it on. She takes after him.* p. 32	**Polite requests and offers** *I'll give you a ride. Do you think you could ...? Can you tell me ...? Would you mind ...?* p. 33
5 Our changing world *page 34*	**Future forms** *Will, going to,* or Present Continuous? *What will the world be like? Things are going to change. We're meeting James at 11:00.* **Future possibilities – may, might, could** *The earth may get warmer. Temperatures might rise. What could happen?* p. 34	**Word building** Suffixes *prediction, excitement* Prefixes *impossible, disagree, react* Changing word stress *iˈmagine / imagiˈnation* p. 40	**Arranging to meet** *I was wondering if we could meet. I'll just get my calendar. We could have coffee. Why don't we ...? Let's ...* **Music of English – making suggestions** p. 41
6 What matters to me *page 42*	**Information questions** *What's she like? What does she look like? How is she?* p. 42 *How tall/big ...? What color/size/brand ...? Which floor/part of town ...? How far/long ...? How much/many ...?* p. 42	**Describing people, places, and things** *He's a lot of fun/very sociable.* p. 42 *It's cozy/on the fourth floor.* p. 43 *What brand is it?* p. 43 **Adjectives** *-ed / -ing: amazing, amazed* Adjective + noun: *sandy beach* Compound adjectives: *well-dressed* p. 44 **Adverbs** *-ly* and not *-ly: simply, fully, just, too* verb + adverb: *wait patiently* p. 45	**In a department store** *Toys and babywear Ladies' fashions Stationery What size do you wear? Keep your receipt.* **Signs** *Buy two, get one free Final clearance* p. 49

Audio Scripts p. 114   **Grammar Reference** p. 129   **Extra Materials** p. 143

SKILLS DEVELOPMENT

READING	LISTENING	SPEAKING	WRITING
Worlds apart *Welcome to our world* The lives of two families from different parts of the world (jigsaw) p. 6	**A world in one family** Ana from Spain and her son, Xavier, talk about living in the U.S. p. 8	**A class survey** Lifestyles p. 5 **Exchanging information** Comparing two families from different parts of the world p. 6 **What do you think?** Discussing the pros and cons of bringing up a family in another country p. 8 **Role play** Acting out everyday situations p. 9	**An informal letter** Correcting mistakes (1) Finding and correcting mistakes in a sample letter *I do mistakes WW* Writing a letter to a friend, correcting each others' letters p. 99
Charles, Prince of Wales *The life of a hardworking future king* – the private and public man p. 14	**Who earns how much?** How much do different jobs pay? p. 13 **Spoken English** – giving opinions *I guess ... I'd say ...* *I think so, too. Actually ...* p. 13	**Talking about you** How often do you do things? p. 11 **Project** Interviewing someone about his/her job p. 12 **Discussion** Which job deserves most money? p. 13 The role of monarchy p. 15 **Exchanging information** Talking about your free time activities p. 16	**Letters and e-mails** Differences in formal and informal writing Beginnings and endings of letters and e-mails *I am writing in response ...* *Give my regards to Robert.* E-mailing an old friend with news p. 100
A Shakespearean Tragedy *Romeo and Juliet* The love story in cartoons p. 22	**The first time I fell in love** Three people talk about their experiences of early love p. 24 **Dictation** Transcribing a summary of an interview p. 20	**A Shakespearean Tragedy** Retelling the story of Romeo and Juliet from pictures p. 22 **What do you think?** Shakespeare and his plays p. 22 Falling in love – Who do we fall in love with? Which couples are well-suited? p. 24	**Telling a story (1)** Two stories: "The farmer and his sons" "The Emperor and his daughters" Linking ideas *as soon as* *However* Writing a folk tale or fairy tale p. 101
Kids then and now *Kids who have it all* Bringing up kids in the 1970s and now p. 30	**Rules for life** Three people talk about their personal philosophies p. 29 **Spoken English** – have got to *I've got to go now. Bye!* p. 29 **Song** *I Believe* by Ian Dury p. 29	**Discussion** Laws in the U.S. and your country p. 28 What's important to you in life? p. 29 **What do you think?** Bringing up children Household rules p. 30	**A biography** Mother Teresa of Calcutta Combining sentences *Her father, who was Albanian, died, leaving her mother to bring up the family.* Researching facts about a famous person and writing a biography p. 102
Life fifty years from now *Life in 2060* An international group of scientists make their predictions p. 38	**World weather warnings** Five weather forecasts from around the world p. 36 **Rocket man** Steve Bennett, scientist and space traveler p. 37 **Spoken English** – pretty *The weather was pretty bad.* p. 37	**Discussion** Talking about changes in the environment p. 35 **What do you think?** Space tourism p. 37 Predictions about the future p. 38 **Role play** Making arrangements to meet p. 41	**Writing for talking** – my cause for concern A speech by a teenager about the influence of video games on children *The thing I'm concerned about ...* *Let me explain why.* Writing a talk about an issue that concerns you p. 103
The heart of the home *My Kitchen* Three women's kitchens in three different countries (jigsaw) p. 46	**My closest relative** Five people talk about who they feel closest to in their family p. 48 **Spoken English** – adding emphasis *My father I don't get along with.* *What I like about her is ...* *The thing I love about him is ...* p. 48	**Project** Your most treasured possession p. 45 **Talking about you** Your kitchen p. 46 **Discussion** First-born/second-born children Who do you feel closest to in your family? p. 48	**Describing a place** – a description of a room **Relative pronouns** *who / that / which* **Participles** *I spend hours listening to music.* Writing about your favorite room p. 104

Word List p. 148   **Verb Patterns and Irregular Verbs** pp. 154–155   **Phonetic Symbols** p. 155

1 A world of difference

Grammar: Tenses: Auxiliary verbs
Vocabulary: What's in a word?
Everyday English: Everyday situations

STARTER

1 Each question has one word missing. Write it in.
   1. Where do you ⁀come from?
   2. When and where you born?
   3. You live in a house or an apartment?
   4. Why you studying English?
   5. Which foreign countries have you been?
   6. What you do last night?
   7. What are you going do after this class?

2 Ask and answer the questions with a partner.

   Where do you come from?
   Mexico.

3 Tell the class about your partner.
   Susana comes from Mexico. She's studying English because...

I DIDN'T KNOW THAT!
Tenses and auxiliary verbs

1 Answer the questions in the *One World Quiz*. Discuss your answers with a partner.

2 **CD1 2** Listen and check your answers. Make notes about the extra information you hear for each one. Discuss this as a class.

> **GRAMMAR SPOT**
>
> 1 Read the questions in the quiz again. Identify the tense in each one. Which two are passive?
>
> 2 Answer these questions. Give examples from the quiz.
>   Which tenses use the auxiliary verbs *do/does/did* to form questions and negatives?
>   Which tenses use the verb *to be* (*is/are/was/were*)?
>   Which use *have/has*?
>
> ▶▶ Grammar Reference 1.1–1.5 p. 129

Write your own quiz

3 Work in two groups.
   • Do some research and write six questions about the world, past and present.
   • Ask and answer the questions with the other group. Which group is the winner?

1 In which country **do** men and women **live** the longest?
   a Japan   b Germany   c The U.S.

2 In which year **did** the world population **reach** 6 billion?
   a 1989   b 1999   c 2005

3 If you **are standing** on the equator, how many hours of daylight do you have?
   a 12   b 16   c 24

4 Where **does** most of the world's oil **come** from?
   a Russia   b Saudi Arabia   c Venezuela

5 Which of the seven wonders of the world **is** still **standing**?
   a The Lighthouse of Alexandria
   b The pyramids of Egypt
   c The Colossus of Rhodes

6 Why **didn't** dinosaurs **attack** humans?
   a Because they were vegetarian.
   b Because they became extinct before humans were on the earth.
   c Because they didn't run fast enough.

7 Where **was** the Titanic **sailing** to when it sank?
   a Southampton   b Rio de Janeiro   c New York

8 How long **has** Hawaii **been** a U.S. state?
   a since 1952   b since 1959   c since 1963

9 How many people **have won** the Nobel Peace prize since it started in 1901?
   a 26   b 58   c 94

10 How long **have** people **been using** the Internet?
   a since 1969   b since 1976   c since 1984

11 Which language **is spoken** by the most people in the world?
   a Spanish   b Chinese   c English

12 In which country **were** women first **given** the vote?
   a Canada   b Paraguay
   c New Zealand

PRACTICE

You're so wrong!

1 Correct the information in the sentences.
   1. The Pope lives in Montreal.
      He doesn't live in Montreal! He lives in Rome.
   2. Shakespeare didn't write poems.
      You're wrong! He wrote hundreds of poems.
   3. Vegetarians eat meat.
   4. The Internet doesn't provide much information.
   5. The world is getting colder.
   6. John F. Kennedy was traveling by plane when he was killed.
   7. Brazil has never won the World Cup.
   8. The 2008 Olympics were held in Tokyo.

2 **CD1 3** Listen and check. Notice the stress and intonation. Practice making the corrections with a partner.

's = *is* or *has*?

3 Is *'s* in these sentences the auxiliary *is* or *has*?
   1. Who's making that noise?   *is*
   2. She's done really well.
   3. My sister's a teacher.
   4. Who's been to Thailand?
   5. He's leaving early.
   6. What's produced in your country?

4 **CD1 4** Listen to some more sentences with *'s*. After each one say if it is *is* or *has*.

Talking about you

5 Complete the questions with the correct auxiliary verb and name the tense.
   1. What time _____ you usually get up on weekends?
   2. What time _____ you get up this morning?
   3. How long _____ it usually take you to get from home to school?
   4. Who _____ sitting next to you? What _____ he/she wearing?
   5. How long _____ you known the teacher?
   6. What _____ you doing when your teacher came into the room?
   7. What _____ (not) you like doing in English class?
   8. Which school subjects _____ (not) you like when you were younger?
   9. Which other foreign languages _____ you studied?
   10. What presents _____ you given on your last birthday?

   Ask and answer the questions with a partner.

Unit 1 • A world of difference   3

MAKING CONVERSATION
Short answers

1 **CD1 5** Ruth is picking up her children, Nick and Lily, from school. Listen and complete the conversation. Which child is more polite? In what way?

Ruth So kids, _____ you have a good day at school?

Nick No.

Lily Yes, I _____. We _____ practicing for the school concert.

Ruth Oh, wonderful! _____ you have a lot of homework?

Lily Ugh! Yes, I _____. I have Geography, Spanish, and Math! _____ you have a lot, Nick?

Nick Yeah.

Ruth Nick, _____ you remember to bring your soccer uniform?

Nick Um …

Lily No, he _____. He forgot it again.

Ruth Oh, Nick, you know we need to wash it. _____ you playing soccer tomorrow?

Nick No.

Ruth Lily, _____ you need *your* uniform tomorrow?

Lily Yes, I _____. I have a softball game after school. We're playing our rival team.

Ruth _____ they beat you last time?

Lily Yes, they _____. But we'll beat them tomorrow.

Nick No, you _____! Your team's terrible.

Ruth OK, that's enough, children. Put on your seatbelts! Let's go!

> **SPOKEN ENGLISH Sounding polite**
>
> 1 In English conversation it can sound impolite to reply with just *yes* or *no*. We use short answers with auxiliaries.
>
>   "Did you have a good day?" "Yes, I did/No, I didn't."
>
> 2 It also helps if you add some more information.
>
>   "Do you have a lot of homework?" "Yes, I do. I have Geography, Spanish, and Math."
>
> 3 Reply to these questions. Use short answers and add some information.
>   1. Did you have a good day?
>   2. Do you like pizza?
>   3. Did you enjoy the movie?
>   4. Has it stopped raining?
>
> ▶▶ Grammar Reference 1.6 p. 129

2 Rewrite Nick's lines in Exercise 1 to make him sound more polite.
CD1 6 Listen and compare the conversations.

3 Work in groups of three. Look at CD1 5 and CD1 6 on page 114. Practice them, sounding polite and impolite.

4 Unit 1 • A world of difference

PRACTICE

1 Match a line in **A** with a short answer in **B** and a line in **C**.

A	B	C
1. Did you hear that noise?	No, I haven't.	They didn't have my size.
2. Are you doing anything tonight?	No, I'm not.	I think it was thunder.
3. Have you seen my cell phone anywhere?	Yes, it is.	Thank goodness!
4. Did you get those shoes you liked?	Yes, I did.	Do you want to come over?
5. Is it time for a break?	No, I didn't.	Did you lose it again?

CD1 7 Listen and check. Practice with a partner. Pay attention to stress and intonation.

A class survey

Find out about the students in your class.

2 Read the class survey and answer the questions about you. Add two more questions.

3 Work with a partner. Ask and answer the questions in the survey. Give short answers in your replies and add some information.

> Are you interested in any sports?

> Yes, I am. I often go skiing in the winter and I like playing tennis.

4 Tell the class about your partner.

> Milo's interested in two sports—skiing and tennis. He often …

5 What can you say about your class?

> Nearly everyone is interested in at least one sport. Most of the boys love football. Some of us like skiing.

Check it

6 There is one mistake in each sentence. Find it and correct it.
 1. Rae comes from Canada and he speak French and English.
 2. Which subjects Susan is studying in school?
 3. "Do you like football?" "Yes, I like."
 4. Did you watched the game last night?
 5. What does your parents do on the weekend?
 6. I think is going to rain.
 7. What was you talking to the teacher about?
 8. I don't think John's arrive yet.

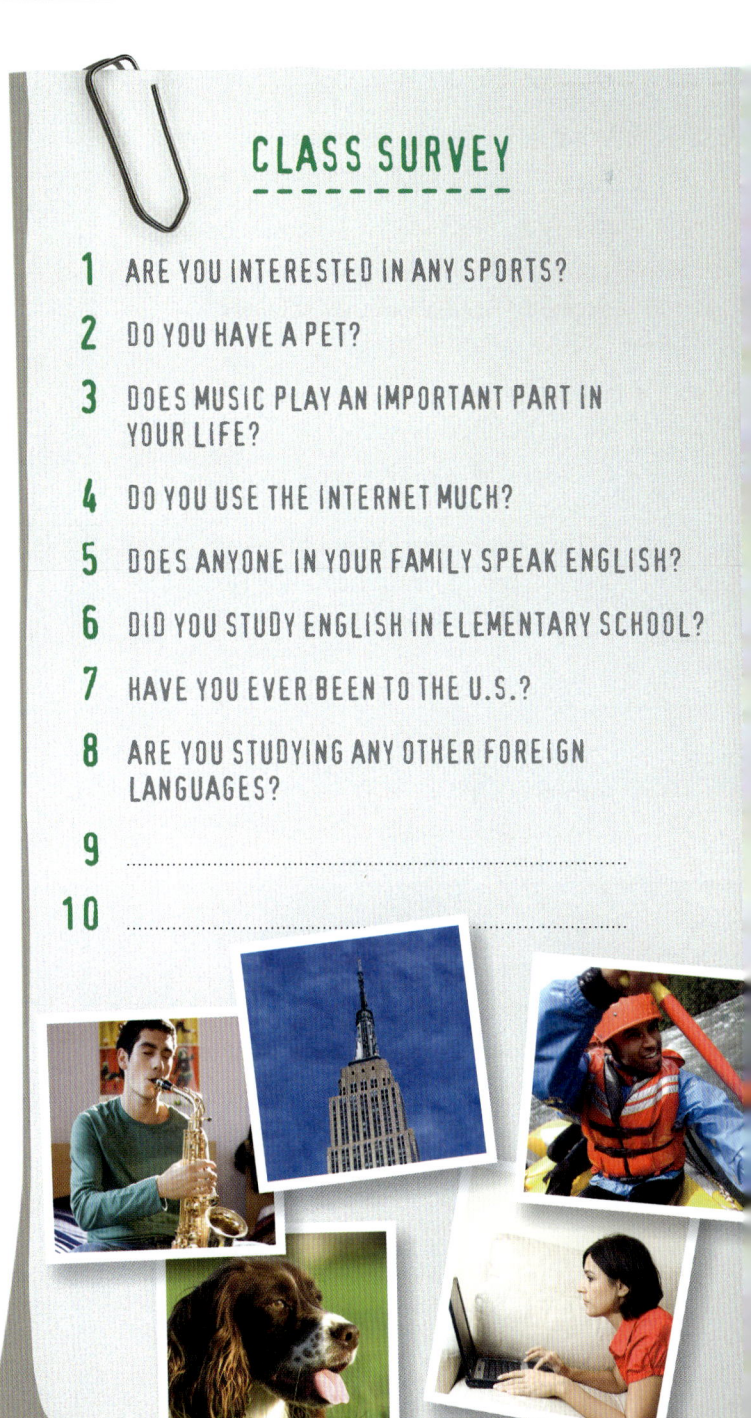

CLASS SURVEY

1 ARE YOU INTERESTED IN ANY SPORTS?

2 DO YOU HAVE A PET?

3 DOES MUSIC PLAY AN IMPORTANT PART IN YOUR LIFE?

4 DO YOU USE THE INTERNET MUCH?

5 DOES ANYONE IN YOUR FAMILY SPEAK ENGLISH?

6 DID YOU STUDY ENGLISH IN ELEMENTARY SCHOOL?

7 HAVE YOU EVER BEEN TO THE U.S.?

8 ARE YOU STUDYING ANY OTHER FOREIGN LANGUAGES?

9 ....

10 ....

Unit 1 • A world of difference 5

READING AND SPEAKING
Worlds apart

1. Discuss these questions about your family.
   - Who is in your immediate family?
   - Name some of your extended family.
   - Who are you close to?
   - Who do you live with now?
   - Who did you grow up with?

2. Read the PROFILES of two families from very different parts of the world. Who is in the family? Where do they come from? What do you know about their countries?

3. Divide into two groups.

   Group A Read about the **Kamau family** from Kenya.

   Group B Read about the **Qu family** from China.

4. In your groups answer these questions about the Kamaus or the Qus.
   1. Where do they live? What are their homes like?
   2. How long have they lived there?
   3. What jobs do the parents do? Do they earn much money?
   4. What do they spend their money on?
   5. What do you learn about the children? What do they do?
   6. How long have the parents known each other?
   7. What do you learn about other members of the family?
   8. What hopes and ambitions do the parents have for themselves and their children?

5. Work with a partner from the other group. Compare and swap information about the families and their mottos.
   1. What similarities and differences can you find?
   2. How have their lives changed over the years?
   3. What regrets or worries do they have now?

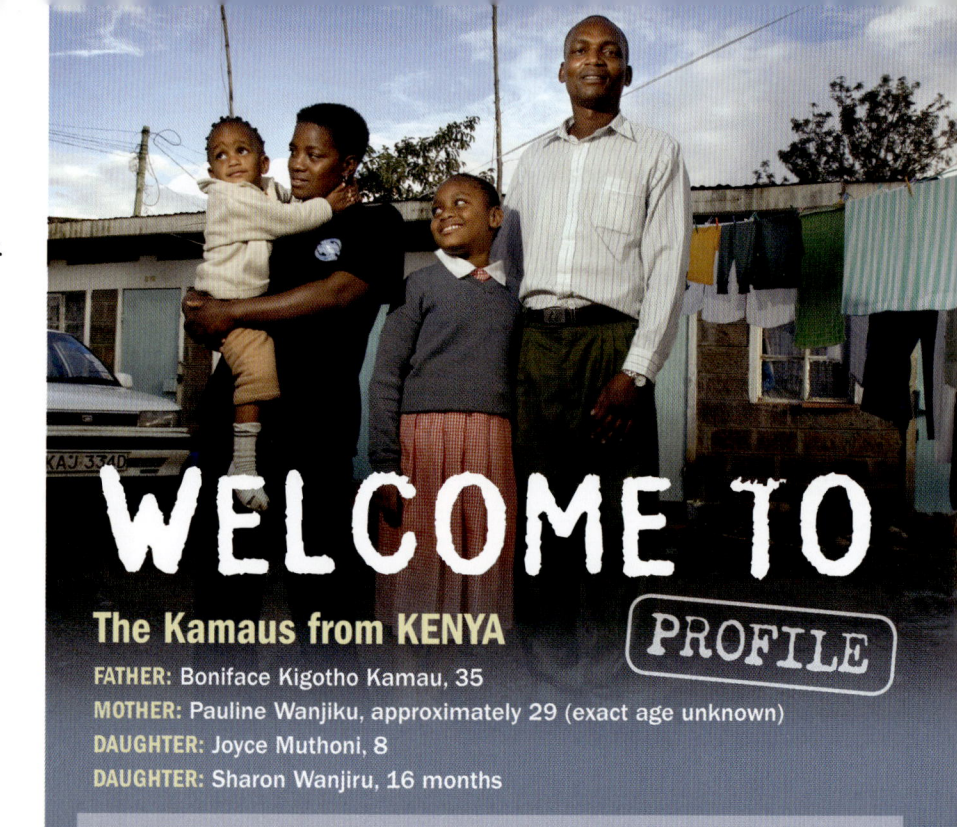

WELCOME TO
PROFILE

The Kamaus from KENYA
FATHER: Boniface Kigotho Kamau, 35
MOTHER: Pauline Wanjiku, approximately 29 (exact age unknown)
DAUGHTER: Joyce Muthoni, 8
DAUGHTER: Sharon Wanjiru, 16 months

Boniface and his wife, Pauline, live in Ongata Rongai, a small town near the capital, Nairobi. They have two daughters: Joyce, who is in her third year of school, and 16-month-old Sharon.

Their home is a two-bedroom apartment, one of 20 in a single-story block. Boniface works as a taxi driver at the international airport in Nairobi. Each morning he leaves home at 4:30 A.M. in his white Toyota—cracked windshield, 200,000 miles on the speedometer—and is back by 10 P.M. On a good day he finds two clients. In a typical month he takes home about $215.

"It's a hard job, but I like it," he says. "I meet new people, so I get some experience of the world—even though I have never been outside Kenya."

Pauline is a dressmaker but isn't working right now. She stays at home to take care of the kids. The weekend is often the only time Boniface sees Joyce and Sharon. Boniface and Pauline met in 1994: "We liked each other immediately," says Boniface. "I didn't want a woman from the city, so when I learned that Pauline was from the country, I was pleased."

They married in 1995, and at first they lived in a slum. They often didn't have a lot to eat, just sukuma wiki (a green vegetable). Then, in 1996, Boniface won $90 in a bicycle race. The money helped them move to a better area and paid for driving lessons so that Boniface could become a taxi driver.

His salary doesn't go far. Rent is $45 a month, and he gives the same amount to his parents, who don't work. Also, as the most successful of six brothers and sisters, Boniface is expected to help their families, too. He says, "I am always so stressed about money." Joyce's school fees cost another $40 a month.

"We are trying to give our children the best education," says Pauline, who, like her husband, never finished school. "Joyce wants to be a doctor."

Next year, Sharon is going to preschool, so Pauline will have more time to start her own dressmaking business. By then, the family might have a new home. "This apartment is not a good place to raise a family," says Boniface. "The bathrooms are communal—one for every four families." Boniface plans to build a three-bedroom house in the suburbs of Nairobi.

THE FAMILY IS HAPPIEST WHEN they have some spare money: Boniface takes them to see the wild animals at Nairobi National Park.
FAMILY MOTTO Try to do your best at all times.

OUR WORLD

The Qus from Beijing, CHINA

PROFILE

FATHER: Qu Wansheng, 44
MOTHER: Liu Guifang, 43
DAUGHTER: Chen, 17
GRANDFATHER: (Qu's father) Huanjun, 84

Qu and Liu have known each other since childhood. The most noticeable change in China since then is the size of families. Qu was the youngest of six. Liu grew up as one of five children. But they have only one daughter.

Qu and Liu are happy to have a girl. Like most parents in China, they put the needs of their only child, Chen, first. She is applying to study at the prestigious Beijing University. Qu, a propaganda officer at the municipal services bureau, and Liu, who works at the No. 3 computer factory, are saving every last yuan for their daughter's education.

The family has lived in their house in central Beijing for 70 years. It is in one of the capital's ancient Hutong alleyways. These areas are known for their close-knit families and warm hospitality. The elderly sit outside and chat. People wander to the stores in their pajamas. It is a way of life cherished by Qu, but he can see that this relaxed routine is increasingly out of step with a nation experiencing one of the most amazingly quick changes in human history.

"We are not in a hurry to get rich," says Qu. "I don't want to rush around trying to make money—I am not a machine. I put my family first."

Tens of thousands of alleyways have been knocked down in the past few years, and their house is said to be next for demolition. And when the old communities go, the traditional family structure, in which children take care of their elderly parents at home, goes too.

But for now, the Qus keep the old ways. The grandfather, Qu Huanjun, 84 and frail, is the center of the family. "My father lives here, so this is the headquarters of the family," says his son. "My brothers and their families come to visit most weekends. We are very close."

They are sad that their daughter has grown up alone because she has no brothers or sisters. "Our daughter is lonely," says Liu. "I always wanted to have two children."

Qu and Liu are proud of their daughter. Chen is bright and well-balanced. She wants to study archaeology. "College will cost a great deal of money," says her father. "So we try to live frugally and save for our daughter."

THE FAMILY IS HAPPIEST WHEN they are all together in the evening.
FAMILY MOTTO Save money, live simply, care for your friends, tell the truth.

Vocabulary work

6 Find the six highlighted words in your text. Work out the meanings from the contexts.

Match the words to the meanings in the chart.

The Kamaus
1. someone who makes clothes
2. with only one floor
3. an area of old houses in bad condition
4. shared by a group of people
5. broken
6. worried

The Qus
1. loved and treasured
2. weak and unhealthy
3. narrow lanes between buildings
4. knocking down buildings
5. close and caring
6. economically

7 Work with a partner from the other group. Teach them your words.

What do you think?

- In what ways are these families typical of their country?
- What is a typical family in your country? Is there such a thing?
- Is your family typical? Why/Why not?

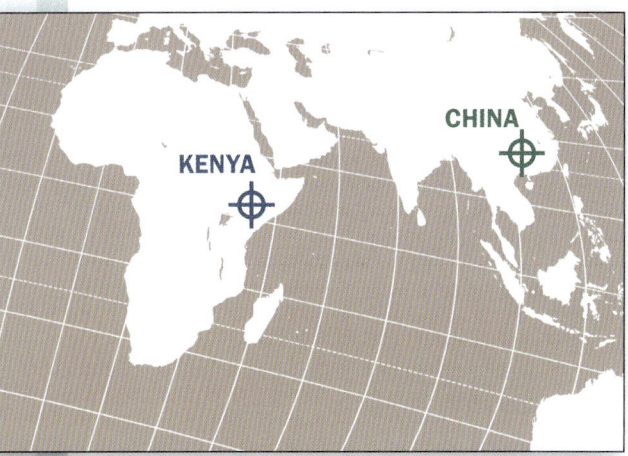

Unit 1 • A world of difference 7

LISTENING AND SPEAKING
A world in one family

1. Do you know anyone who has married someone of another nationality? Do they have any children? Tell the class.

2. Look at the photo of the family. There are *three* nationalities in the family. How can this be?

3. **CD1 8** Listen to Xavier talking about his family. Read and answer the questions. <u>Underline</u> any you cannot answer.
   1. What nationality are Xavier and his parents, Ana and Teo? Which city do they live in?
   2. How did Xavier's parents meet? Give details. Why did they decide to live in the U.S.?
   3. When and why did Xavier first notice his nationality?
   4. Why weren't Xavier and James bilingual as children?
   5. How many times has Xavier been to Spain? How old was he? How many times has James been?
   6. What contact does Xavier have with his father's family? How long did Xavier and his family stay in Peru every summer?
   7. What is Xavier studying? What is James going to study?
   8. What is Xavier hoping to do in the future? Where is he planning to live?
   9. What is James doing right now? What's he going to do?
   10. What does Ana think are the pros and cons of bringing up a family in another country?

4. **CD1 9** Now listen to Xavier's mother, Ana. Answer the questions that you <u>underlined</u> in Exercise 3.

What do you think?

- What are the pros and cons of bringing up a family in another country? Make two lists.

   + You get the best from two cultures   − You don't feel completely at home in either of them

- Discuss your lists as a class.

8 Unit 1 • A world of difference

VOCABULARY
What's in a word?

These exercises will help you to think about how you learn vocabulary.

Meaning

1. These sentences all contain the nonsense word *uggy*. Is *uggy* used as a **verb**, an **adjective**, a **noun**, or an **adverb**?
   1. My grandmother's very old and *uggy* now so she can't get out much.
   2. She gave me my grandfather's gold watch. I'll *uggy* it forever.
   3. The poor people lived crowded together in *uggies* in the old part of the city.
   4. They can't afford to buy meat and fish. They live very *uggily* on rice and potatoes.

   Can you guess what *uggy* means in the four sentences?
   Which real English word goes into each sentence?
   • cherish • frail • slums • frugally

Pronunciation

2. Say these words aloud. <u>Underline</u> the word with the different vowel sound.
   1. /oʊ/ or /ʌ/   rose goes does toes
   2. /i/ or /eɪ/   meat beat great street
   3. /eɪ/ or /ɛ/   paid made played said
   4. /ʌ/ or /oʊ/   done phone son won

   CD1 10 Listen and check.

   Phonetic symbols *p. 155*

3. Say these words aloud. Which syllable is stressed?

   mother enjoy apartment
   holiday **population**

   CD1 11 Listen and check.

Word formation

4 Complete the word *act* in the sentences using the suffixes from the box.

| -ress | -ion | -ing | ~~-ive~~ | -ivities |

1. My grandfather is 84, but he's still very act **ive** .
2. My sister's an act_____. She's often on TV.
3. Act_____ is not always a well-paid job.
4. This is not a time to do nothing. It is a time for act_____.
5. We do a lot of act_____ in class to learn English.

Words that go together

5 Match a word in **A** with a line in **B**.

A	B
cosmopolitan	carelessly
well-paid	city
close-knit	in love
drive	a race
fall	family
win	job

Keeping vocabulary records

6 Discuss how you can keep vocabulary records.
- Do you have a special notebook or do you record your vocabulary electronically?
- Do you write a sentence with the new word?
- Do you write the translation? What about pronunciation?

📌 My notes

records /ˈrɛkərdz/ *noun*
a written note of something
• *I keep vocabulary records.*

record /rɪˈkɔrd/ *verb*
to write down or keep information electronically
• *I record my vocabulary electronically.*

▶ **WRITING** AN INFORMAL LETTER *p. 99*

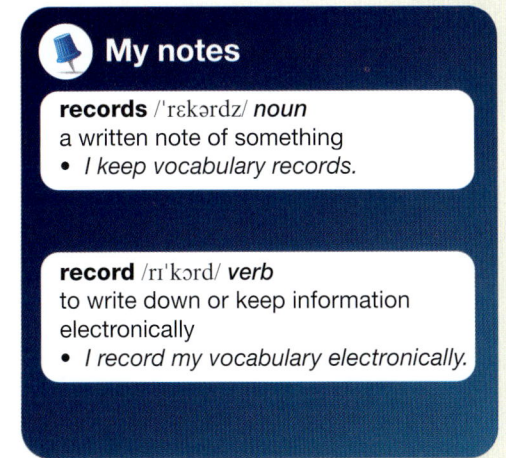

EVERYDAY ENGLISH
Everyday situations

1 Work with a partner. Where could you hear the following lines of conversation? Who is talking to who?

1. I need to make an appointment. It's pretty urgent. I've lost a filling.
2. A medium latte and a muffin, please.
3. I can't make the meeting. I'm stuck in traffic.
4. Can you put in your PIN number and press "Enter"?
5. Bottled or tap? And do you want ice and lemon in it?
6. I don't think you've met Greg. He's joining us from our New York office.
7. How many bags are you checking in?
8. The elevator's on your right. Would you like someone to help you with your luggage?
9. Please hold. Your call is important to us. All our operators are busy at the moment, but one of them will be with you shortly *(music)* …
10. There are still tickets for the 5:45 performance, but the 8:45 performance is sold out, I'm afraid.

2 Match a line from Exercise 1 with a reply.
a. **7** Just the one.
b. ☐ Don't worry. We'll start without you and brief you later.
c. ☐ Hello. Good to meet you. I've heard a lot about you.
d. ☐ No, thank you. I'll manage.
e. ☐ That's fine. We'll have two, please, one adult, one child.
f. ☐ For here or to go?
g. ☐ Oh, no! I can't remember my number for this card. Oh, what is it?
h. ☐ If I have to listen to that again, I'll go crazy!
i. ☐ Bottled, please. Ice but no lemon.
j. ☐ We have a cancellation this afternoon. 2:45, if that's OK?

CD1 12 Listen and check. How does each conversation end?

3 Listen again. Pay attention to the stress and intonation. Practice some of the conversations with your partner.

Role play

4 Work with a partner. Turn to page 143 and act out the situations.
CD1 13 Listen and compare.

Unit 1 • A world of difference 9

2 The work week

Grammar: Present tenses • Passive
Vocabulary: Free time activities
Everyday English: Making small talk

Blue Monday, how I hate Blue Monday

STARTER CD1 14 Listen to the song called **"Blue Monday."**
- What is the singer's favorite day of the week?
- What's wrong with the other days?
- Which days are OK?

MY FAVORITE DAY OF THE WEEK
Present tenses – states and activities

1 Look at the photos.
What do the people do? What are they doing?
In pairs, ask and answer questions.

What does Vicky do? *She's a student.*
What's she doing? *She's doing her homework.*

2 CD1 15 Listen to them talking about their favorite day of the week. What is it? Why?

Vicky's favorite day of the week is . . . because she . . .

3 Listen again and complete the sentences.

1. I _____ with my parents during the semester.
2. I _____ day today.
3. … it _____ work at all. Time _____ by.
4. The restaurant _____ redecorated right now …
5. I _____ because it's challenging, but I _____ surfing.
6. The boards _____ here in the U.S.
7. We never _____ on weekends or holidays …
8. Now we're harvesting, so we _____ at all.

What else can you remember about each person?

Vicky likes being with her friends all the time.

4 Work with a partner. What is your favorite and least favorite day of the week? Why?

10 Unit 2 • The work week

GRAMMAR SPOT

1. What are the tenses in these sentences? Why are they used?

   I **have** two classes on Monday.
   I'**m having** a bad day today.

   Find more examples, active and passive, in **CD1 15** on p. 115.

2. Which of these verb forms is right? Why is the other wrong?

   | I like | my job. | I know | we're very lucky. |
   | I'm liking | | I'm knowing | |

   Some verbs are rarely used in Continuous tenses. These are called stative verbs. Underline the five stative verbs in the box.

   love   understand   work   want   enjoy   cost   need   learn

3. Adverbs of frequency (*always, never*) answer the question *How often?* Find examples in **CD1 15** on p. 115.

▶▶ Grammar Reference 2.1–2.4 pp. 130–1

Dave Telford
police officer and surfer

PRACTICE

Questions and answers

1. Read about Dave, the police officer from page 10. Which question goes with which paragraph?

   How often do you go surfing?   What do you think of your job?
   ~~What's your background?~~   Do you have a business?
   Why do you like surfing?   What hours do you work?
   What is your favorite day of the week?

   CD1 16 Listen and check.

2. Complete the questions about Dave. Then ask and answer them with a partner.

   Where does he live?   **In Los Angeles, California.**

   1. Where . . . he live?
   2. . . . he married?
   3. Why . . . morning shift?
   4. How many hours . . . ?
   5. What . . . like about his job?
   6. What . . . think . . . while . . . surfing?
   7. Where . . . next month?
   8. . . . business doing well?
   9. What . . . on Sunday evenings?

   CD1 17 Listen and check.

TALKING ABOUT YOU

3. Make sentences about *you* using the prompts in the box.
   I visit friends as often as I can.

. . . as often as I can.	Sometimes I . . .
. . . eight hours a day.	. . . one night a week.
. . . when I'm on vacation.	. . . twice a year.
. . . on Sunday.	I hardly ever . . .
I always . . .	. . . whenever I'm not working.

4. Talk to a partner about you. Tell the class about your partner.

---

1 | What's your background? |

I'm 35, and I'm single. I live in Los Angeles, California. I'm a police officer. I've been in the police force for over ten years. I love my job, but my passion is surfing.

2

I work different shifts. The morning shift starts at 5:00, and I can't stand that because I have to get up at 4:30. My favorite shift is 2:00 in the afternoon until midnight because I get home about 12:30. What's good is that I work ten hours a day for four days, then have three days off.

3

My job is extremely busy and very hard. But I like it because it's challenging, and I never know what's going to happen. I like working in a team. We look after each other and work together.

4

My work is very stressful, so I surf to get away from it all. It's just me and the sea, and my mind switches off. I concentrate so hard on what I'm doing that I don't think about anything else.

5

I go surfing whenever I'm not working. Sometimes I'm on the beach before 7:00 in the morning. I go all over the world surfing. Next month I'm going to Costa Rica, and in the fall I'm going to Thailand.

6

I have a surfing school. I teach all ages, from kids to seniors. The business is doing well. I'm also opening two shops that sell surfboards. The boards are made here in the U.S.

7

I like Sundays best of all. I work as a lifeguard all day, then around 6:00 me and my friends barbecue some burgers and relax. Awesome! I've been all around the world, but when I look around me, I think there's nowhere else I'd rather be.

THE OFFICE

Simple and continuous

1 **CD1 18** Listen to two people talking about who's who in "The Office." What are their names? What are their jobs?

d	Simon	Accountant
	Edward	*Human Resources (HR) Manager*
	Anna	Managing Director (MD)
	Jenny	**Personal Assistant (PA)**
	Matthew	Information Technology (IT) Manager
	Christina	*Sales Director*

2 What are the people doing? What are they wearing?

Simon's sitting at the head of the table reading something. He's wearing a sweater.

CD1 18 Listen again. What comment is made about each person?

Simon shouts a lot, but he listens, too.

3 Match a job from Exercise 1 with a job description and a current project.

The MD is responsible for running the whole company. Currently, he is ...

Job description	Current project
is responsible for running the whole company	buying new hardware
makes appointments and arrangements	*making bookings for a conference*
negotiates prices and contracts	**visiting new customers in China**
runs an IT support team	recruiting new staff
is in charge of budget and cash flow	*discussing plans and targets with the Board*
deals with employees	preparing a financial report

4 Work with a partner. Read the conversation aloud.

A What's your job?
B I'm a Human Resources Manager.
A So what do you do exactly?
B I deal with employees and their training.
A And what are you working on right now?
B I'm recruiting and interviewing. We're trying to find new staff for our office in Tokyo.

5 Make similar conversations using the jobs in Exercise 1. Choose another job, for example, film director, journalist ...

PROJECT

Interview someone you know about his/her job. Tell the class about this person.

I talked to ..., who's a ... He ..., and he starts work at ... He has to ... He likes his job because ... On his days off he ...

STATE AND ACTIVITY VERBS

6 Are these sentences right (✓) or wrong (✗)? Correct the wrong sentences.

1. I'm not wanting an ice cream.
2. Are you understanding what I'm saying?
3. I'm enjoying the class. It's great.
4. I'm thinking you're really nice.
5. What are you thinking about?
6. I'm not believing you. You're telling lies.
7. I'm knowing you're not agreeing with me.
8. She's having a lot of money.

12 Unit 2 • The work week

ACTIVE AND PASSIVE

7 Read the statistics. Choose the correct form, active or passive. Do any of the statistics surprise you?

STATISTICS ABOUT JOBS AND MONEY IN THE U.S.

1. Nearly half the population (155m) **involve / are involved** in some form of employment.
2. More than 1.8 million people **employed / are employed** by the government.
3. The average worker **pays / is paid** $42,000 a year.
4. The average single worker **pays / is paid** 23.6% of his salary in taxes.
5. Women **earn / are earned** on average 12% less than men for full-time work.
6. Children **give / are given** on average $10 a week allowance money.
7. The average person **spends / is spent** $70 per week on transportation.
8. The average household **owns / are owned** two cars.

▶▶ Grammar Reference 2.5–2.6 p. 131

8 Put the verbs in the present passive, simple or continuous.
1. "Can I help you?" "I'<u>m being helped</u> (help), thank you."
2. A lot of manufactured goods _____ (make) in Asia.
3. "Why are you taking the bus?" "My car _____ (service)."
4. A large percentage of the food we buy _____ (import).
5. The banking industry in the U.S. _____ (situate) in New York.
6. _____ the tip _____ (include) in the bill?
7. The hotel is closed while the bedrooms _____ (remodel).
8. Basketball players _____ (pay) far too much money.

LISTENING AND SPEAKING
Who earns how much?

1 Work with a partner. Look at the chart. Discuss which job you think goes with which salary.

Who earns how much in the U.S.? *

$30,000 $200,000   **$1 million**

$140,000   Doctor   Basketball player $25,000
Senior Director   Nurse
Teacher   Supermarket cashier
$20,000   Police officer   Pilot $65,000
Lawyer   Farmer

$40,000 $750,000
$48,000

* The average annual salary is $42,000.

2 You are going to hear two people discussing the chart.
CD1 19 Listen to **Part 1**. Answer the questions.
1. Which jobs do they discuss? Which salaries do they agree on?
2. Complete the sentences.
They think a doctor earns either $_____ or $_____.
They think either a _____ or a _____ earns $750,000.
They think a _____ earns about $65,000.
3. What comment do they make about … ?
• doctors   • basketball players   • senior directors   • pilots

3 **CD1 20** Listen to **Part 2**. Answer the questions.
1. Who do they think are the lowest earners?
2. How much do they think farmers earn?
3. Do they agree about a teacher's and a police officer's salary?
4. What is the woman's final point?

SPOKEN ENGLISH   Giving opinions

1. Notice the ways of expressing an opinion.
   I guess …   I'd say …   I suppose …
   Find three more in CD1 19 and CD1 20 on p. 116.
2. Are these ways of agreeing or disagreeing?
   I think so, too.   Definitely.   I know what you mean, but …
   I'm not so sure.   Actually, …   Absolutely.
3. What do we mean when we say … ?
   Could be.   Maybe, maybe not.   Possibly.
4. Discuss the salary chart again using some of these expressions.

---

4 Work in small groups. Turn to page 143. Which salaries do you think are unfair? Are any surprising?

Unit 2 • The work week   13

READING AND SPEAKING
Charles, Prince of Wales

1. Do you know the names of the people on the balcony? What is the relationship between them?

2. Work with a partner. Write down what you know about Prince Charles. Compare your ideas as a class.
   He's about 60.
   He's heir to the British throne.

3. What do you think occupies most of his time? Write a number from 0–5 next to each activity with 0 = not at all and 5 = a lot.
   ___ earning a living
   ___ hunting
   ___ entertaining
   ___ traveling
   ___ skiing
   ___ performing royal duties
   ___ being with his family

4. Read the article. Answer the questions after each part.

   Part 1
   1. What gives you the impression that Charles is extremely wealthy?
   2. What happens to his staff if they do well? What happens if they don't?

   Part 2
   3. What is the routine when he entertains?
   4. What is the private side of Prince Charles?

   Part 3
   5. What are some of his public duties?
   6. What good deeds does he do?

   Part 4
   7. "Prince Charles has everything." What does he have? What doesn't he have?
   8. What is Duchy Originals? What is happening to it? What does it sell?
   9. In what different ways is Charles referred to?
   future King   Prince of Wales . . .

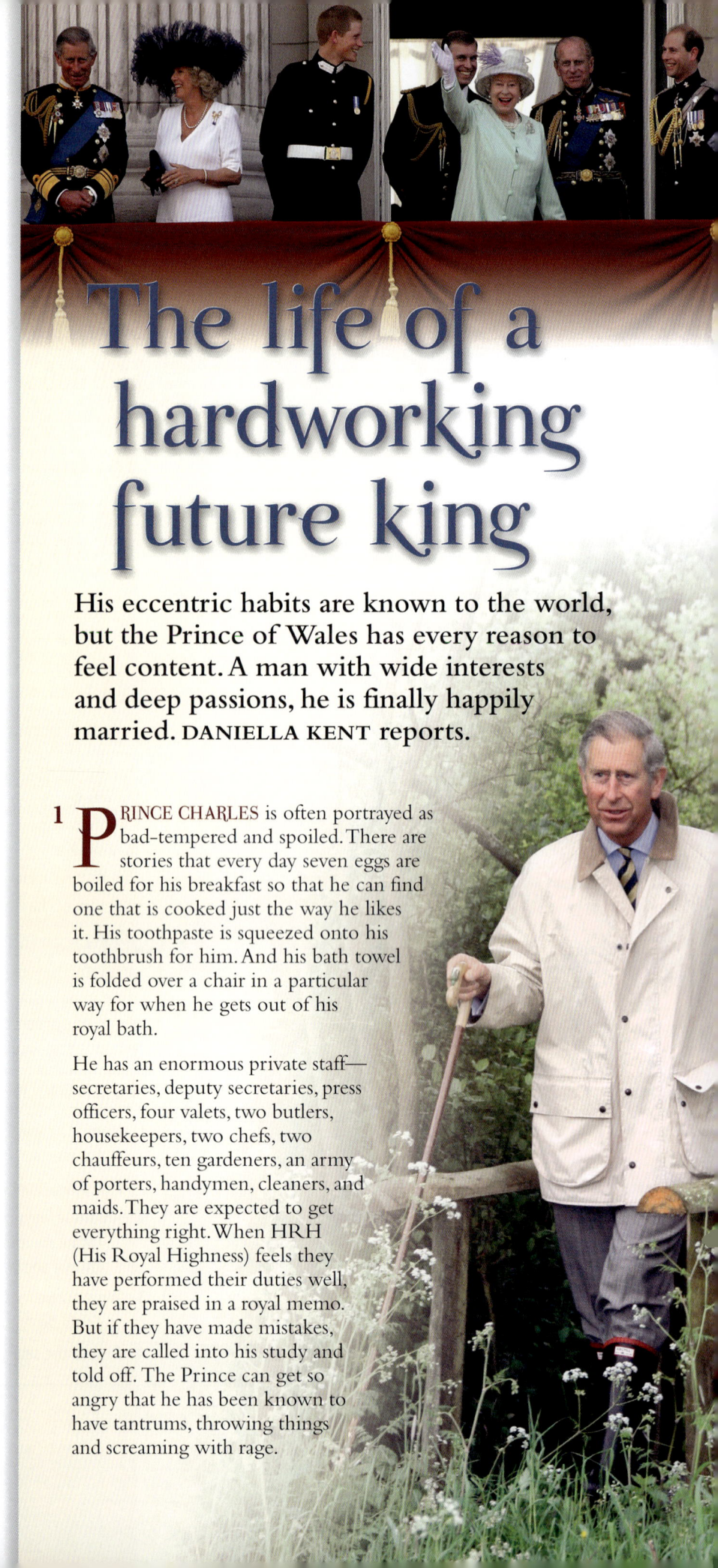

The life of a hardworking future king

His eccentric habits are known to the world, but the Prince of Wales has every reason to feel content. A man with wide interests and deep passions, he is finally happily married. DANIELLA KENT reports.

1 PRINCE CHARLES is often portrayed as bad-tempered and spoiled. There are stories that every day seven eggs are boiled for his breakfast so that he can find one that is cooked just the way he likes it. His toothpaste is squeezed onto his toothbrush for him. And his bath towel is folded over a chair in a particular way for when he gets out of his royal bath.

He has an enormous private staff—secretaries, deputy secretaries, press officers, four valets, two butlers, housekeepers, two chefs, two chauffeurs, ten gardeners, an army of porters, handymen, cleaners, and maids. They are expected to get everything right. When HRH (His Royal Highness) feels they have performed their duties well, they are praised in a royal memo. But if they have made mistakes, they are called into his study and told off. The Prince can get so angry that he has been known to have tantrums, throwing things and screaming with rage.

14 Unit 2 • The work week

The private and public man

2 Charles is eccentric, and he admits it. He talks to trees and plants. He wants to save wildlife but enjoys hunting, shooting, and fishing. He dresses for dinner, even if he's eating alone. He's a great socializer. Poets, artists, writers, broadcasters, politicians, actors, and singers all eat at his table. Arriving at Highgrove, his family home, on a Saturday afternoon, guests are entertained in the height of luxury. They are then sent on their way before lunch on Sunday, having been shown around his beautifully-kept gardens.

The Prince also entertains extravagantly at Sandringham, one of the Queen's homes, at least twice a year. There are picnic lunches on the beach, expeditions to local churches, and lavish dinners with organic food. Conversation is lively, but the heir to the throne has to be careful what he says, because he knows only too well that anything he says in private may be repeated in public.

The future monarch that we don't see is a man of great humor who cares passionately about the state of the British nation and is devoted to his two children, William and Harry. He is madly in love with "his darling wife," which is how he refers to Camilla in public.

A dutiful life

3 Together Charles and Camilla perform royal duties, both at home and abroad. He attends over 500 public engagements a year. He visits hospitals, youth groups, performing artists, charities, and business conferences. He hosts receptions to welcome visiting heads of state and VIPs. He travels abroad extensively, as an ambassador to the United Kingdom, representing trade and industry. He works hard to promote greater understanding between different religions. He is also President of the Prince's Charities, which are active in promoting education, business, the environment, the arts, and opportunities for young people. The group raises over £110 million annually.

Camilla shares Charles's passion for hunting and also his interest in conservation of towns and countryside. The one thing she leaves to Charles is skiing. She prefers to stay at home when he makes his annual trip to Klosters in Switzerland.

Everything except the top job

4 Since his second marriage, Prince Charles has everything he wants, except, as his first wife Diana (who was killed in a car accident in 1997) used to call it, "the top job." Yet despite not being on the throne, he has worked hard to accomplish so much. He is concerned about the state of the country he loves and is frustrated that governments do little to tackle those problems about which he feels so strongly.

The Prince of Wales has his own food company, Duchy Originals. It originally sold cookies, but it is now expanding to become one of Britain's best-known and most successful organic brands, with over 200 different products, including food, drinks, and hair and body care products.

Charles, well-intentioned, hardworking, conservative, and old-fashioned, continues to do his duty as he sees it. But he is no longer alone. One day he will be King, and his darling Camilla will be at his side.

5 Now that you have read the article, have you changed your mind about any of your answers in Exercise 3?

VOCABULARY WORK

Which of these adjectives are positive and which are negative?

hardworking – positive

~~hardworking~~	bad-tempered	
spoiled	eccentric	old-fashioned
sociable	cautious	passionate
frustrated	successful	well-intentioned

Give an example of Charles's life or behavior that illustrates each adjective.

hardworking – He performs a lot of royal duties and does charity work.

DISCUSSION

- What do you know about the attitude of the British people to their royal family?
- What countries do you know that have a royal family? Are the members of the family popular? What do they do?

Unit 2 • The work week 15

VOCABULARY AND SPEAKING
Free time activities

1 What do you do when you aren't working? Make a list of what you do in your free time.

go on the Internet   play golf   go for a run

Who do you do it with? Where? Tell the class.

2 What activities can you see in the photos? Which of them …?
  - do you do alone, or with another person
  - do you do at home, or in a special place
  - needs special clothes or equipment

3 Which of these things go with the activities?

a drill	a recipe
planting	serving an ace
sales	a sleeping bag
a racket	a screwdriver
a concert	a bargain
zoom	staying fit
sweating	meditating
wearing a helmet	a flashlight
sketching	weeding

4 Complete the diagram about cooking with words from the box.

boiling	to chop
to mix	a baking dish
herbs and spices	ground beef
an oven	baking
roasting	a food processor
olive oil	to weigh

5 Choose an activity that you are interested in. Draw a similar diagram and choose the categories. Fill it in.

6 **CD1 21** Listen to John talking about his hobby. Make notes under these headings.
  - Favorite hobby
  - Where and when he does it
  - Clothes and equipment
  - What he likes about it
  - The best part

7 Work in small groups. Use the headings from Exercise 6 and your diagram to talk about what you like doing in your free time.

equipment
a saucepan

ingredients
eggs

cooking

food preparation
to peel

ways of cooking
frying

16 Unit 2 • The work week

EVERYDAY ENGLISH
Making small talk

1 When do we make small talk? Who with? What about?

2 **CD1 22** Read and listen to the conversation between Ann and Joaquim. Where are they? What is Joaquim doing there?

Ann	So, what do you think of Chicago, Joaquim?
Joaquim	*really interesting/great city/beautiful buildings/people so friendly* It's really interesting. Chicago's such a great city. There are some beautiful buildings, and the people are so friendly!
Ann	Yes, they are! When did you get here?
Joaquim	*… ago/flight from Miami/a bit late/didn't matter*
Ann	Oh, good. Where are you staying in Chicago?
Joaquim	*… Avenue Hotel/convenient for the office/room not very big/OK*
Ann	That's too bad! Don't worry. Where are you from?
Joaquim	*Brazil/born in São Paulo/live in a suburb of Rio de Janeiro/pretty/sea*
Ann	Really? It sounds beautiful. Your English is very good. Where did you learn it?
Joaquim	*… very kind/a lot of mistakes/school for years/been to the U.S. many times*
Ann	Oh, have you? How interesting! And what are you doing here in Chicago, Joaquim?
Joaquim	*… attending a conference/here for five days/home on the 17th*
Ann	Oh, so soon! And have you managed to get around our city yet?
Joaquim	*… not seen very much/a walk along the lakefront path/taken a boat tour from the Navy Pier/not seen the John Hancock Observatory yet*
Ann	Well, I hope you enjoy it. Don't work too hard!
Joaquim	*… try to enjoy myself/bye/nice to talk*

3 What information does Joaquim add to keep the conversation going? How does Ann show she's interested? Find examples.

4 Work with a partner. Use the prompts to practice the conversation.
CD1 22 Listen again. How well did you do?

SPOKEN ENGLISH Softening a negative comment

1 In conversation, we sometimes don't want to sound too negative. We soften negative comments.

We were late landing.   We were **a bit** late landing.
My room is tiny.   My room **isn't very big**, but it's OK.

2 Make these comments softer. Use the words in parentheses.
1. It's expensive. *(bit)*
2. It's hard. *(quite)*
3. It's cold. *(warm)*
4. They're rude. *(friendly)*
5. I earn very little. *(much)*
6. There's nothing to do. *(very much)*

5 **CD1 23** Listen to the questions and answer them. Make a comment and add some information. Add a question if you can.

> Who do you work for?

> Siemens. I've been with them for four years. They're a good company. How about you?

CD1 24 Listen and compare.

6 You are abroad on a business trip. Invent a name and a background for yourself.

You are at a social event. Stand up and socialize! Ask and answer questions.

▶▶ **WRITING** LETTERS AND E-MAILS *p. 100*

3 Good times, bad times

Grammar: Past tenses
Vocabulary: Spelling and pronunciation
Everyday English: Giving opinions

STARTER Play the *Fortunately, Unfortunately* game as a class.
Start: I woke up very early this morning.
Student A   Fortunately, it was a beautiful day.
Student B   Unfortunately, I had to go to school.

VINCENT VAN GOGH
Past tenses and *used to*

1 Look at the pictures by the painter Vincent Van Gogh. What do you know about him? Was he happy? Was he successful?

2 Read the notes below about Vincent Van Gogh. Complete the questions about his life.

Vincent Van Gogh
1853–1890

Vincent Van Gogh was born in 1853. When he was a young man he worked in London and Paris, but he was fired.
He tried to commit suicide.
In Paris, Vincent met many famous artists while he was ✱.
In 1888 he moved to Arles in the south of France. Another famous painter came to live with him. He was an old friend.
One evening Van Gogh left the house carrying a ✱. He cut off part of his ear.
After this, he moved into an asylum. Many of his most famous paintings were completed here.
In 1890, while he was ✱, he shot himself in the chest. Two days later he died. He was buried. When he died, he had no money.

1. Where **was he born**?
2. What ... job?
3. Why ...?
4. Why ...?
5. Which ...?
6. What ... when he met them?
7. Who ...?
8. Where ... first meet?
9. What ...?
10. Why ...?

11. Which ...?
12. What ... doing ...?
13. Why ...?
14. Where ...?
15. Why didn't ...?

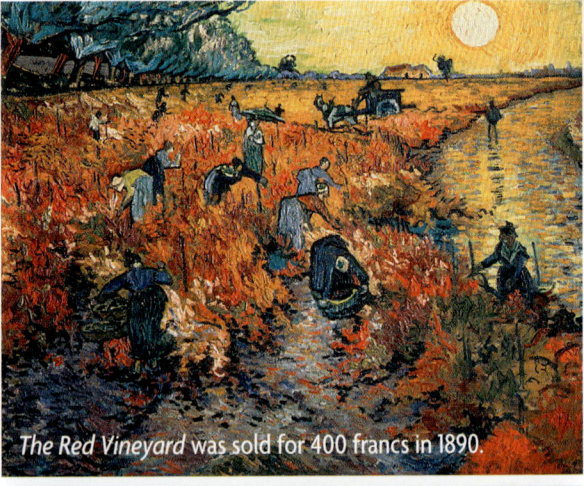

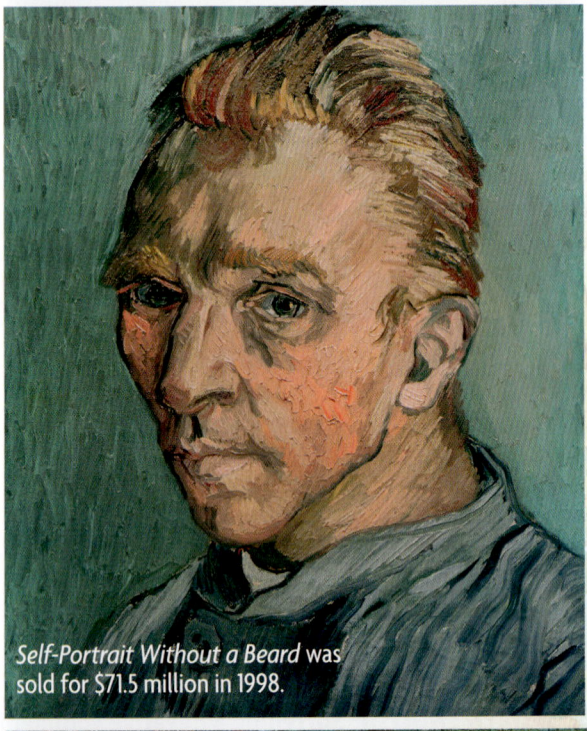

CD1 25 Listen and check the questions.

The Red Vineyard was sold for 400 francs in 1890.

Self-Portrait Without a Beard was sold for $71.5 million in 1998.

Irises was sold for $53.9 million in 1987.

18 Unit 3 • Good times, bad times

3 Read the complete text about Vincent Van Gogh. With a partner ask and answer the questions from Exercise 2.

CD1 26 Listen and check.

Vincent

Vincent Van Gogh, the genius unrecognized in his own lifetime

Vincent Van Gogh was born in Brabant in the Netherlands in 1853. As a young man he worked as an art dealer in London and Paris. He was fired from this job because he had argued with customers about art.

In 1881 he tried to commit suicide. He was depressed because he had fallen in love with his cousin, but she had rejected him.

In 1886 he went to Paris to study art, and it was while he was studying that he met Degas, Pissarro, Seurat, Toulouse-Lautrec, Monet, and Renoir.

After two years in Paris, Van Gogh went to live in Arles in the south of France. His friend and fellow painter, Gauguin, who he had met in Paris, came to join him. The two men settled down in Arles, but there was a lot of tension between them. They used to quarrel fiercely, mainly about the nature of art.

One evening in December 1888, Van Gogh left the house carrying a razor blade. He'd been arguing with Gauguin again and was very distressed. He cut off part of his ear.

After this, he moved voluntarily into an asylum for the insane at St-Rémy-de-Provence. He used to wake up at six in the morning and go out to paint. It was here, in the last two years of his life, that many of his most famous paintings were completed. These included *Starry Night*, *Irises*, and *Self-Portrait Without a Beard*.

In 1890 he left the warm south and moved to Auvers-sur-Oise. Here he continued working despite his growing depression. It was while he was painting outside that Vincent shot himself in the chest. Two days later, he died. He was buried in the cemetery in Auvers.

When Van Gogh died, he had no money because he'd only sold one of his paintings, *The Red Vineyard*, in his entire life. His sister-in-law took his collection to Holland, where his work was published. He was instantly recognized as a genius.

GRAMMAR SPOT

1 In these sentences, which verb form is ...?
   Past Simple   Past Continuous   Past Simple passive

   He **worked** as an art dealer.
   He **was fired**.
   He **was studying** art.

   Find more examples of the three verb forms in the text.

2 In this sentence, what happened first?

   He **was fired** because he **had argued** with customers.

   had argued is an example of the Past Perfect tense.
   How is this tense formed? Find more examples in the text.

3 Look at the sentence.

   Vincent **used to** wake up at six.

   Do you think this happened once or many times?
   Find another example of *used to* in the text.

▶▶ Grammar Reference 3.1–3.7 pp. 131–3

Pronunciation

4 **CD1 27** Listen and repeat the weak forms and contracted forms.

/wʌz/   /wʌz/
What was he doing?   He was studying.

/wɹ/   /hɪd/
They were working ...   He'd had an argument.

/ðeɪd/   /hɪd bɪn/
They'd met in Paris.   He'd been arguing.

5 Write the verbs from the box in the chart according to the pronunciation of *-ed*.

| ~~worked~~ tried rejected |
| completed continued died |
| published recognized moved |

/t/	/d/	/ɪd/
worked		

CD1 28 Listen and check.

Unit 3 • Good times, bad times 19

PRACTICE

I didn't do much

1. **CD1 29** Listen to four people saying what they did last night. Who said these lines? Write a number from 1–4.
   - ___ I went out to eat with a couple of friends.
   - ___ We talked for a while.
   - ___ I didn't do much.
   - ___ I got home about nine.
   - ___ I had an early night.
   - ___ I didn't get home until about midnight.
   - ___ I did some stuff on the computer.
   - ___ It was a very late night for me!

2. What did *you* do last night? Discuss in small groups.

Discussing grammar

3. Compare the use of tenses in these sentences. Say which tense is used and why.
   1. It | *rained* all day yesterday.
         | *was raining* when I woke up.
   2. I *wore* a suit for my interview.
      She looked great. She *was wearing* a black top and new jeans.
   3. "What *were* you *doing* when you lost your phone?"
      "Shopping."
      "What *did* you *do* when you lost your phone?"
      "Bought a new one."
   4. When Bill arrived, | we *were having* lunch.
                         | we *had* lunch.
                         | we'*d had* lunch.
   5. I got to the theater. The movie | *started*.
                                       | *had started*.
   6. When I was a kid I *used to play* football with my dad.
      I *played* football with my kids last Saturday.

A newspaper story

4. Read the newspaper article. Put the verbs in parentheses in the correct past tense, active or passive.
   CD1 30 Listen and check.

5. **CD1 31** Listen to a radio news item on the subject of the same accident. What do you learn that wasn't in the newspaper article?

SMASH!
Clumsy visitor destroys priceless vases
By Tom Ball

A CLUMSY visitor to a local museum has destroyed a set of priceless 300-year-old Chinese vases after slipping on the stairs.

The three vases, which (1)_____ (produce) during the Qing dynasty in the 17th century, (2)_____ (stand) on the windowsill at the City Museum for forty years. Last Thursday they (3)_____ (smash) into a million pieces. The vases, which (4)_____ (donate) in 1948, (5)_____ (be) the museum's best known pieces.

The museum (6)_____ (decide) not to identify the man who (7)_____ (cause) the disaster. "It was a most unfortunate and regrettable accident," museum director Duncan Robinson said, "but we are glad that the visitor (8)_____ seriously _____ (not injure)."

The photograph (9)_____ (take) by another visitor, Steve Baxter. "We (10)_____ (watch) the man fall as if in slow motion. He (11)_____ (fly) through the air. The vases (12)_____ (explode) as though they (13)_____ (hit) by a bomb. The man (14)_____ (sit) there stunned in the middle of a pile of porcelain when the staff (15)_____ (arrive)."

The museum declined to say what the vases were worth.

VOCABULARY
Spelling and pronunciation

1 **CD1 32** Listen and repeat these words. What do they tell you about English spelling and pronunciation?

good /gʊd/   food /fud/   blood /blʌd/
road /roʊd/   rode /roʊd/   rowed /roʊd/

Words that sound the same

2 **CD1 33** Listen and write the words you hear. What do they have in common? Compare with a partner. Did you write the same words?

3 Read these words aloud. Write another word with the same pronunciation.

1. male	mail	6. week	_____
2. blew	_____	7. hole	_____
3. piece	_____	8. pair	_____
4. where	_____	9. allowed	_____
5. sun	_____	10. weight	_____

4 Write the correct spelling of the words in phonemic script.

1. /pis/ Peace is the opposite of /wɔr/_____.
2. I'm not /əlaʊd/_____ to /wɛr/_____ make-up.
3. I'd like a /pɛr/_____ of /blu/_____ jeans, please.
4. I /wɔr/_____ the same socks for a /hoʊl/_____ /wik/_____.
5. I had to /weɪt/_____ in the rain and I caught the /flu/_____.

Spelling

5 Read these words aloud. Which two words rhyme?

1. (love)	move	(glove)
2. some	home	come
3. dear	fear	pear
4. lost	most	post
5. meat	cheat	great
6. boot	shoot	foot
7. eight	weight	height
8. blood	wood	flood
9. flower	power	lower

CD1 34 Listen and check.

6 These words have the same vowel sound but different spellings. Spell the words.

/u/ t_oo_th   tr_u_th   j___ce   thr___
/ɔ/ c___t   d___n   w___r   fl___
/ər/ ___th   w___ld   b___n   f___
/ɛr/ t___   f___   squ___   th___

Lost sounds

7 In some words we lose sounds.

chocolate /tʃɑklət/ has two syllables, not three.
comfortable /kʌmftəbl/ has three syllables, not four.

Read these words aloud. Cross out the lost sounds.

different   several
business   restaurant
marriage   interesting
vegetable   temperature

CD1 35 Listen and check.

8 Some words have silent letters. Cross out the silent letters in these pairs of words.

1. foreign   sign
2. climb   bomb
3. neighbor   weigh
4. honest   hour
5. knee   knock
6. psychology   psychiatrist

CD1 36 Listen and check.

Unit 3 • Good times, bad times

READING
A Shakespearean tragedy

1. What do you know about William Shakespeare?

2. Look at the list of characters in the story of *Romeo and Juliet*. What do you know about the story? How did people at that time decide who to marry? Who made the decision?

3. Read 1–5 in the story. Answer the questions.
   1. Why did the Montagues and the Capulets hate each other?
   2. Why wasn't it a good idea for Romeo to go to the Capulets' party?
   3. What happened when Romeo and Juliet first met?
   4. "Wherefore art thou Romeo?" (= Why are you Romeo?) Why was Juliet upset about Romeo's name?
   5. How long had they known each other when they decided to get married?
   6. Why did Friar Laurence agree to marry them?
   7. Why did Romeo try to stop the fight?

4. Read 6–9 in the story. Answer the questions.
   1. Who did Juliet go to for help?
   2. What was the Friar's plan?
   3. Which part of the plan worked?
   4. What went wrong with the plan?
   5. Why did Romeo kill himself?
   6. Why did Juliet kill herself?
   7. How did their families feel at the end?

5. **CD1 37** Listen to actors speaking Shakespeare's lines, and follow them in the story. Read the lines in more modern English on page 144.

6. Retell the story using the pictures.

What do you think?
- Whose fault was the tragedy?
- In the play, Romeo and Juliet fall in love at first sight. Do you think this is too soon to fall in love?
- Shakespeare wrote comedies, tragedies, and history plays. What titles do you know? Do you know any of the stories?

▶▶ **WRITING** TELLING A STORY (1) **p. 101**

22 Unit 3 • Good times, bad times

Romeo

The Montagues

Lord Montague — *Romeo, son of Montague* — *Mercutio, Romeo's best friend*

> Peace! I hate the word As I hate hell, all Montagues and thee!

1 Many years ago, in the ancient Italian city of Verona, there were two very rich but warring families, the Montagues and the Capulets. They had hated each other for so long that no one could remember how the feud had started. Fights often used to break out in the streets.

> My heart's dear love is set on the fair daughter of rich Capulet.

> ...This alliance may so happy prove, to turn your households' rancour to pure love.

4 The next morning, Romeo raced to Friar Laurence and begged him to marry them. The Friar agreed, hoping this would unite the families. That afternoon, Juliet joined Romeo, and they were wed. They parted, but planned to meet again that night.

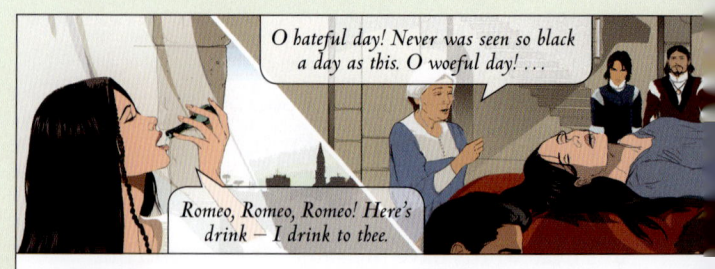

> O hateful day! Never was seen so black a day as this. O woeful day!...

> Romeo, Romeo, Romeo! Here's drink – I drink to thee.

7 Juliet returned home and took the drug. The next day, everyone thought she was dead. She was carried to the family tomb, from where, according to the Friar's plan, Romeo would rescue her.

AND Juliet by William Shakespeare

The Capulets

- Benvolio, Romeo's cousin
- Friar Laurence, a priest
- The Prince
- Paris, a nobleman suitor of Juliet
- Juliet's nurse
- Tybalt, Juliet's cousin
- Juliet, daughter of Capulet
- Lord Capulet

2 Lord Capulet was planning a celebration for his daughter, Juliet. Romeo, Lord Montague's son, went to the party uninvited. He saw Juliet and fell instantly in love! They touched hands. They talked. Only then did they discover their families were enemies!

Did my heart love till now? For I ne'er saw true beauty till this night.

My only love sprung from my only hate, ...

3 That night, Juliet stood on her balcony and declared her love for Romeo. Romeo had climbed up a wall and was listening. They swore eternal love to each other, and promised to marry in secret the next day.

O Romeo, Romeo, wherefore art thou Romeo? Deny thy father, and refuse thy name ... What's Montague? ... A rose by any other name would smell as sweet.

5 Returning to Verona, Romeo found Benvolio and Mercutio being attacked by Tybalt. Romeo tried to stop the fight. He failed, and Mercutio was killed. Romeo had to take revenge! He fought Tybalt and killed him. The Prince, hearing of the deaths, banished Romeo from Verona.

Now, Tybalt, ... Mercutio's soul is ... above our heads, either thou or I, or both, must go with him.

Thou wretched boy ... shalt with him hence.

6 More disaster was to come. Juliet's father had decided she should marry a nobleman, Paris. How could she tell her father she had already married Romeo? Juliet ran to Friar Laurence for help. The Friar gave her a sleeping potion to make her appear dead. The Friar would tell Romeo to arrive as she was waking up. They could then escape together.

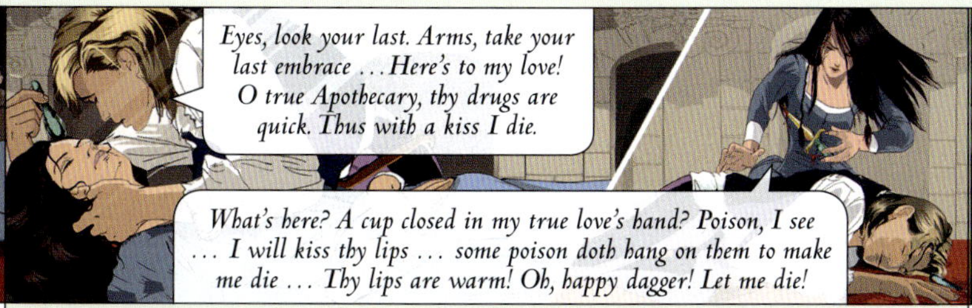

Take thou this vial, ... and this liquor drink ... no pulse ... no breath shall testify thou livest ... two and forty hours ...

Give me! ... Love give me strength.

8 But Romeo never received the Friar's letter. Thinking that his beloved Juliet had died, he bought poison and went to the tomb. He kissed her and drank the poison. Juliet woke up to see Romeo lying dead beside her. She wept and kissed him, hoping that the poison would kill her, too. Finally, she took his dagger and stabbed herself.

Eyes, look your last. Arms, take your last embrace ... Here's to my love! O true Apothecary, thy drugs are quick. Thus with a kiss I die.

What's here? A cup closed in my true love's hand? Poison, I see ... I will kiss thy lips ... some poison doth hang on them to make me die ... Thy lips are warm! Oh, happy dagger! Let me die!

9 The families of the Montagues and the Capulets arrived at the tragic scene. They were overwhelmed with grief, and horrified at the pain that their families' hatred had caused. Thus they buried their feud, along with their precious children, Romeo and his sweet Juliet.

For never was a story of more woe than this of Juliet and her Romeo.

LISTENING AND SPEAKING
The first time I fell in love

1 What do you think these quotations mean?

- "People ask what love is. If you have to ask, you don't know."
- "Love is a kind of madness."
- "Love is blind."
- "When you're in love, 1 + 1 = everything, and 2 − 1 = nothing."
- "Love is what is left when being in love has burned away."
- "Love is the most beautiful of dreams and the worst of nightmares."

2 **CD1 38** Listen to three people talking about the first time they fell in love. Take notes and complete the chart.

	Sarah	Tommy	James
1. How old was he/she?			
2. Who did he/she fall in love with?			
3. Was it a pleasant experience?			
4. Was the love reciprocated?			
5. How did it end?			

3 In groups, compare your answers. Listen again to check.

4 What are some of the effects of being in love that the people describe?
"He made me go all weak at the knees."

What do you think?

- Who do we fall in love with? Someone like ourselves, or someone different? Do opposites attract?
- "The course of true love never did run smooth." (Shakespeare – *A Midsummer Night's Dream*)
  Think of couples, perhaps famous, perhaps not, who didn't have or haven't had an easy romance. What happened to them?
- What couples do you know who are well-suited? Why do they go well together?

Unit 3 • Good times, bad times

EVERYDAY ENGLISH
Giving opinions

1 **CD1 39** Read and listen to the conversation. What is it about? Which two people agree with each other?

   A So, what do you think of Meg's new boyfriend? He's really great, isn't he?
   B Definitely! I think he's absolutely wonderful!
   A Mmm. Me too. I just love the stories he tells.
   B So do I. He's very funny. I really like his sense of humor.
   A They get along so well, don't they?
   C Well, maybe. He's very nice, but I don't think that he's the one for her.
   B That's not true! They absolutely adore each other!
   C Mmm. I'm not so sure.
   B Come on! You're just jealous. You've always liked her.
   C Actually, that's not true at all. But I really like her sister.

   In groups of three, practice the conversation.

2 Listen again to the conversation. Answer the questions.
   1. A and B agree with each other. What are their actual words?
   2. A uses two question tags. Practice them.

   He's really great, isn't he?
   They get along so well, don't they?

   Is A *really* asking for information, or does she just want the others to agree with her?

3 Complete these question tags.
   1. We had a great time in Thailand, *didn't we* ?
   2. The weather was great, _____?
   3. The French really love their food, _____?
   4. It's a lovely day today, _____?
   5. Karen and Tom are a really nice couple, _____?
   6. Tom earns so much money, _____?
   7. They want to get married, _____?

   CD1 40 Listen and check.

> **SPOKEN ENGLISH** Making an opinion stronger
>
> 1 Adverbs like *very*, *really*, *just*, and *absolutely* help make an opinion stronger.
>   It's good. → It's **very** good. → It's **really** good.
>   It's bad! → It's **just** awful! → It's **absolutely** awful!
> 2 We can use an adverb to qualify an adjective or a verb.
>   He's **really great**, isn't he?
>   I **really don't like** his sense of humor.
> Find more examples in the conversation in Exercise 1.

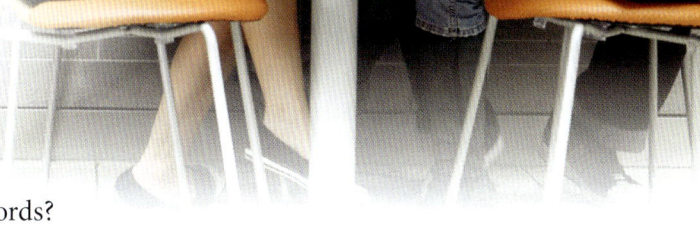

4 Work in pairs to make these opinions stronger. Use a wide voice range to sound enthusiastic.

   1. She's very nice.   *She's absolutely wonderful!*
   2. The movie was good.   *just great*
   3. The hotel's all right.   *really fabulous*
   4. I like dark chocolate.   *absolutely adore*
   5. I like Peter.   *really love*
   6. The book wasn't very good.   *absolutely awful*
   7. I don't like noisy restaurants.   *just can't stand*

   CD1 41 Listen and repeat.

5 Write down some opinions on …
   - the last movie you saw
   - something in today's news
   - the weather
   - the clothes that someone is wearing today
   - what a celebrity is currently doing
   - a show on TV

6 In pairs, ask for and give opinions.

   I saw that new movie last week.
   Oh! What did you think of it?
   Great! I really enjoyed it. The acting was just amazing!

Unit 3 • Good times, bad times   25

4 Getting it right

Grammar: Modal and related verbs
Vocabulary: Phrasal verbs (1)
Everyday English: Polite requests and offers

STARTER

Look at the sentences. Say them aloud as a class.

You	can / must / should / have to	go.

1. Say the negative.
2. Say the question.
3. Say the 3rd person singular with *he*.
4. Which verb is different in form?

MODERN DILEMMAS
should/must/have to/be allowed to

1 Work in groups. *The Times* newspaper has a section called *Modern morals* where readers help other readers with problems. Read the problems in *Readers ask*. What advice would you give? Use these phrases:

I think they should ...   I don't think she should ...   He must ...

2 Read the lines from *Readers reply* on page 27. Which lines do you think go with which problems?

Read the full replies on page 145. Do you agree with the advice?

3 Look again at *Readers ask* 1–7. Find the questions used to *ask for* advice. Find the verbs used in *Readers reply* a–g to *give* advice.

Modern morals

Readers ask

1 How should I deal with my difficult and disagreeable neighbor? He is in the habit of dumping his garden waste along the public sidewalk between our two houses.
Jim T. via e-mail

2 Is it OK to greet people you don't know with a "How are you?" In California (my home) it's considered friendly, but here in New York some people react with a cold look. Should I be less friendly in my greetings?
Erica Fleckberg, New York

3 My new PC automatically picks up wireless networks to gain access to the Internet. This includes the one belonging to my neighbor. Is it right for me to use it?
Richard Dalton, via e-mail

4 My stepfather's driver's license was suspended for six months for speeding, but we have learned that he still drives over the speed limit all the time. Should we keep quiet or inform the police?
Stella Milne, Connecticut

5 I am a medical student. After I graduate in June, I have one month before my first job starts. My fiancée says that I am not allowed to claim unemployment benefits for this month. I disagree, because I'll be unemployed. The benefits are for all those who are out of work, isn't it? What do you think?
J. R. Collin, via e-mail

6 Is it wrong for me to record CDs borrowed from my local library? I am not denying anyone the money, as I wouldn't buy the CD anyway.
Pete Rodriguez, via e-mail

7 Is it ever permissible to lie to children? I lied to my two-year-old granddaughter to remove her from a fairground ride without a tantrum. I said: "You must get off now because the man is going to get his dinner." She got down without a fuss. But I'm worried that if she remembers this, she won't trust me in the future.
Barbara Hope, Philadelphia

26 Unit 4 • Getting it right

GRAMMAR SPOT

1. These sentences give advice. Which is the stronger advice?
   - You **should** check online.
   - You **must** tell your neighbor.

2. Which sentences express permission? Which express obligation?

   | I | can
am allowed to
must
have to | go. |

3. Complete the sentences with *have to*, *don't have to*, or *shouldn't*.
   - Children _____ go to school.
   - You _____ ride your bike on the sidewalk.
   - People over 65 _____ go to work.

4. The past of these sentences is the same. What is it?
   - I must go.   I have to go.

▶▶ Grammar Reference 4.1–4.5 pp. 133–4

Readers reply

a You must call "Crimestoppers" and report him. You don't have to give your name.

b I think you are allowed other benefits. You should check online.

c You don't have to be like New Yorkers just because you're in New York.

d You have to act with self-control. I don't think you should confront him.

e It's not only wrong, it's illegal. You are not allowed to do this.

f Not only should you lie sometimes, you often have to.

g You must tell your neighbor this. It's the only right thing to do.

PRACTICE

Discussing grammar

1 Choose the correct verb to complete the sentences.
   1. I don't get along with my boss. Do you think I *should / must* look for another job?
   2. We're throwing Tom a surprise birthday party. You *shouldn't / can't* tell him about it.
   3. Please, Dad, *can / must* I go to Tom's party? It'll be great.
   4. You *should / have to* drive on the left in England.
   5. Do you *must / have to* wear a uniform in your job?
   6. Are you *can / allowed to* take cell phones to school?
   7. I *must / had to* go to bed early when I was a child.
   8. You *shouldn't / don't have to* go to the U.S. to learn English, but it's a good idea.

   CD1 42 Listen and check.

Giving advice

2 **CD1 43** Listen to the three conversations. After each one discuss these questions.
   1. What is the problem?
   2. What is the advice?
   3. Do you agree with it? Give *your* advice if it's different.

3 Listen again and complete the lines with the exact words.
   1. I don't know if I _____ go or not.
   2. They told her she _____ to have friends over while they were away.
   3. Oh, come on! You _____ come. It's a party.
   4. Look. You _____ tell your mom and dad.
   5. You're _____ to eat in the store.
   6. Do you think I _____ tell her to stop?
   7. No, no, you _____ say anything.
   8. I _____ say something.
   9. I _____ go to the store for my dad.
   10. I think he _____ pay the fine.

Practice the conversations in **CD1 43** on page 118.

Unit 4 • Getting it right   27

Rules present

1 Work with a partner. Read these American laws. Compare them with laws in your country. Are they the same?

In the U.S. ...
1. You can get married when you're 18.
2. In most states, you can't drive a car until you are 16.
3. You must be at least 18 to vote.
4. You have to wear a seat belt in the front seat of a car.
5. In some states, you can't use a cell phone while driving.
6. Young people don't have to do military service.
7. In many states, children aren't allowed to ride a bicycle without a helmet.
8. Children at most private schools have to wear uniforms.

2 What other laws are there in your country? Think of places such as roads, parks, government buildings, libraries, and schools. Tell the class.

Rules past

3 Read "American Education 1840–1918." Use what you find out to choose the correct verb form in the statements.

1. Before 1840, children *had to/didn't have to* go to school.
2. By 1870 people *had to/didn't have to* pay to go to school.
3. By 1900, many children *had to/weren't allowed to* go to school until they were 14.
4. By 1918, most children *weren't allowed to/didn't have to* leave school until they were 16.

4 Look at "One-room Schools." Which of the rules do you think were true? Discuss with a partner. Complete the rules with *had to/didn't have to/weren't allowed to*.

American Education 1840–1918

Nineteenth century American education is often called "The Common School Period." It was during this time that education became available to "common" people. In the 1840s, school attendance became compulsory for elementary-age children, aged 5–12. By 1870, every state provided free elementary education. By 1900, 31 states required children aged 8–14 to attend school. As a result, 72% of American children attended school by 1910—half of them in one-room schoolhouses. By 1918, most states passed laws making education compulsory until age 16.

One-room Schools

1 Students of all ages ___had to___ share one teacher and one classroom.
2 The youngest children _____ sit in front, close to the teacher.
3 Boys and girls _____ sit together.
4 Teachers _____ hit their students.
5 Students _____ do very much homework.
6 Students _____ take an oral test at the end of the school day.
7 Children _____ go to school all year round.
8 Teachers _____ live with local families.

LISTENING AND SPEAKING
Rules for life

1 **CD1 44** Listen to three people talking about their rules for life and make notes after each one.

Millie, 15

Richard, 33

Frank, 65

2 Discuss their ideas. Are they optimists or pessimists? Do you agree or disagree?

> **SPOKEN ENGLISH** *have got to*
>
> 1 *Have got to* means the same as *have to* but is used more in spoken English. In American English *have got to* is an intensive form of *have to*. It's often reduced to *gotta* when we speak. Look at these examples from CD1 46.
>
> You **'ve got to** give meaning to your life by what you do.
> You **'ve got to** look for the good in people.
>
> 2 Complete the conversations with *'ve got to/'s got to*.
>
> 1. "Isn't your mom away this week?"
>   "Yeah, so Dad **'s got to** do all the cooking."
> 2. "Where's my briefcase? I _____ go to work."
>   "It's where you left it. In the hallway."
> 3. "Mom, why can't I go out now?"
>   "You _____ clean up your room first."
> 4. "Won't you be late for work?"
>   "Oh, no! Look at the time. I _____ go now. Bye!"
>
> **CD1 45** Listen and check. What extra information do you hear in the answers? Practice the conversations.
>
> ▶▶ **Grammar Reference 4.2 p. 133**

Song – "I Believe"

3 Look at the photo and read about Ian Dury. Who was he?

Ian Dury (1942–2000) was an English rock and roll singer, songwriter, and bandleader whose career took off during the late 1970s, during the **punk** era of rock music. He is best known as founder and lead singer of the band **Ian Dury and the Blockheads**.

4 **CD1 46** Listen to the song called "I Believe." It expresses Ian's philosophy on life. Is he an optimist or a pessimist?

5 Work with a partner. Turn to page 146. Read the song. Discuss which words best complete the lines.

6 **CD1 46** Listen again and check your answers. Which of the things in 1–8 does he believe in?
1. Recycling trash.
2. Healthy outdoor activities.
3. Having a lot to eat and drink.
4. Being truthful and kind.
5. Having strong opinions about everything.
6. Good manners.
7. Putting yourself first.
8. Peace, not war, is possible.

7 Which of the things in Exercise 6 are important to you? Discuss as a class.

▶▶ **WRITING** A BIOGRAPHY *p. 102*

READING AND SPEAKING
Kids then and now

1. Close your eyes and imagine your bedroom when you were 10. What was in it? Were there many electronic items? Tell the class about your room.

2. Read the introduction to the newspaper article on page 31. Answer the questions.
   1. What did a child's bedroom use to be like?
   2. Why is the bedroom of today's child like a space station?
   3. Why is it sometimes the most expensive room in the house?
   4. What question is asked at the end of the introduction? What is your opinion?

3. The main part of the article describes a modern-day family in an experiment done by a TV company. Look at the photo and the heading. Who are the people? What do you think the experiment was?

4. Here are some words from the article. Use them to predict each paragraph. Check new words in a dictionary.

   Paragraph 1:
   21st century family   Jon made a fortune
   large house   huge bedrooms   hi-tech toys

   Paragraph 2:
   Jon's childhood   small apartment
   mother died   five kids   share household chores

   Paragraph 3:
   back to the 70s   house stripped of all gadgets
   wash own clothes   battered old van $65 a week

   Paragraph 4:
   temper tantrums   Hannah's wardrobe emptied
   Josh – piano, no TV

   Paragraph 5:
   learned to appreciate small treats
   baked cookies   started to save

5. Read paragraphs 1–5 quickly. Were your ideas correct?

6. Read to the end of the article. Answer the questions.
   1. How did Jon make a fortune?
   2. How was Jon's childhood different from his children's?
   3. In what ways was his father strict?
   4. How did the TV company transform their lives?
   5. What did Hannah and Josh have to do that they didn't have to do before?
   6. How did the kids react to the changes at first? How did their attitude change?
   7. How did the kids make extra money?
   8. What is Jon's advice to other parents?

Vocabulary work

Read the sentences below. Find the phrasal verbs in the text which mean the same as the words in **bold**.
1. Electronic items **increase** the value of the rooms.
2. The father, Jon, **founded** his own business.
3. He was one of five children **raised** by his father, when his mother died.
4. Josh had to **stop** watching his widescreen television and **start** taking piano lessons.
5. They enjoyed the meals they'd **cooked** themselves.
6. We shouldn't **surrender** to our kids' demands.

What do you think?

Discuss in groups.
- Do you think a lot of children are spoiled these days?
- What household rules do you think are a good idea for families?
  You must always make your bed.
  Everyone has to help at meal times.

Write a list of rules and read them to the class.

Kids who have it all

GO BACK JUST THIRTY YEARS and look inside a child's bedroom. What do you see? Some books, a few dolls or toy cars, some stuffed animals, and perhaps a desk. Look inside the bedroom of today's kids and it's a 21st century space station.

Computers and other hi-tech toys can make a youngster's bedroom the most expensive room in the house. But it's not only electronic items that push up the value. Today's children also have sports equipment, designer clothes, and accessories such as sunglasses, watches, and jewelry. Do they have everything and appreciate nothing? A TV channel tried an experiment. TANYA BOWERS REPORTS

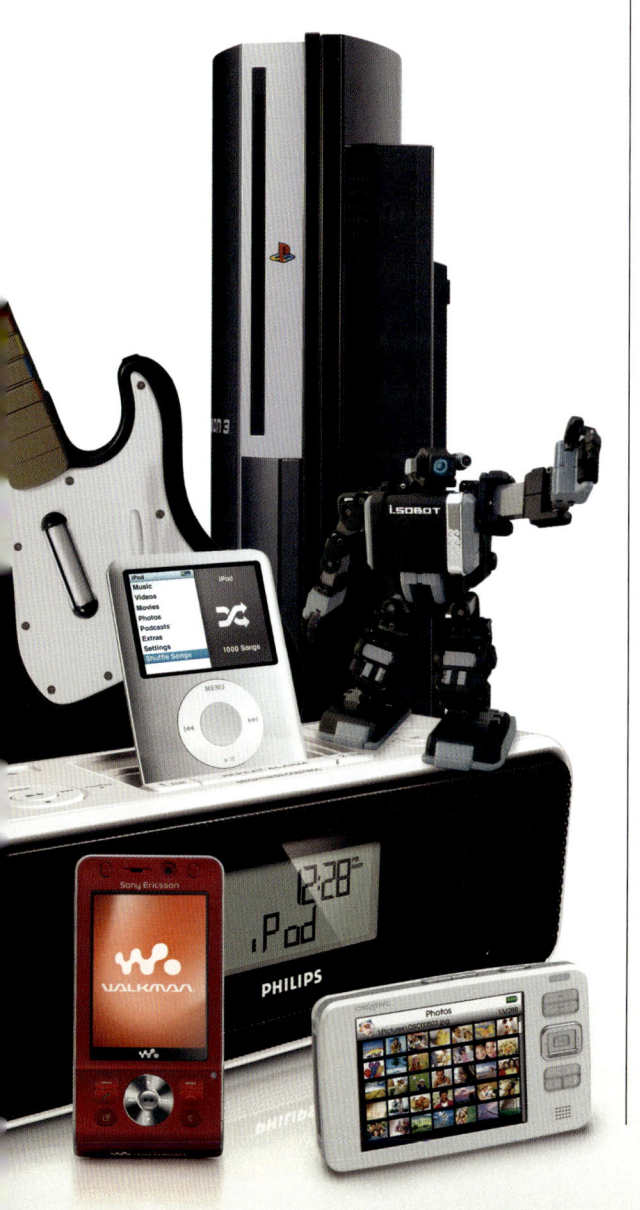

Back to the 1970s

1. The popular reality TV show "It's Your Life" transported a typical 21st century family back in time to the 1970s. The Gregory family lives in a large house in New Jersey. Fifteen years ago the father, Jon, set up his own business and made a fortune. The children, Hannah, 12, and Josh, 10, have huge bedrooms full of expensive hi-tech toys and clothes. They don't have to help at all with the running of the house.

2. This is all very different from Jon's childhood in the 70s. He grew up in a small apartment in Newark, one of five children brought up by their father after his mother died. Discipline, order, and thrift ruled his life. "We ate what we were given. We walked to school and we had to share all the household chores. We had to do what we were told. Dad was very strict."

3. The TV show transformed the Gregorys' house and their lives. For two weeks the family had to go back to the 70s and live Jon's childhood. The house was stripped of all modern gadgets and equipment. Hannah and Josh had to wash and iron their own clothes, do the dishes, and help clean the bathroom. The family car was traded in for a battered, old VW van, and they had to live on just $65 a week.

4. At first there were temper tantrums as the children tried to adjust. Hannah couldn't believe that she wasn't allowed to buy hair mousse and was horrified to find her closet emptied, leaving her with jeans, two shirts, and a formal dress. Josh had to give up watching his widescreen television and take up the piano. They didn't have to walk to school but were filled with embarrassment when their dad drove them to the school in their "new" van.

5. However, gradually Hannah and Josh learned to appreciate small treats. They enjoyed eating the meals they'd put together themselves. They made some extra money by selling cookies they'd baked to their neighbors. They started to save rather than spend and understand the value of a $150 pair of sneakers.

What should today's parents do?

It's difficult to get things right as a parent. Jon says: "We shouldn't give in to our kids' demands. There's no feeling like getting something you've worked really hard for." Hannah now has $50 in the bank, all earned by doing extra jobs around the house. She has learned some valuable lessons about life and she doesn't buy hair mousse anymore!

VOCABULARY AND SPEAKING
Phrasal verbs (1)

Literal or idiomatic meanings?

1 Look at the cartoons. Which two meanings of *take off* are idiomatic? Which is literal?

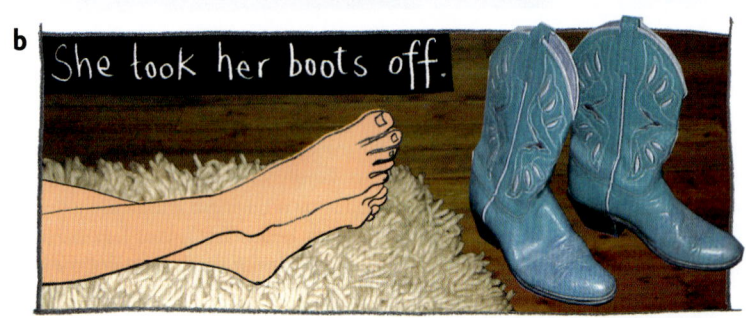

a *His business has really taken off.*

b *She took her boots off.*

c *The flight to Singapore took off on time.*

2 In these groups of sentences which two phrasal verbs are idiomatic? Which is literal?
1. a. He *brought up* five children on his own.
   b. The porter will *bring* your bags *up* to your room.
   c. She *brought up* the subject of money.
2. a. Do you think you'll *get through* your final exam?
   b. I tried to call you but I couldn't *get through*.
   c. His van couldn't *get through* that narrow gate.
3. a. The water was *cut off* because she didn't pay the bill.
   b. Hello, hello? I can't hear you. I think we've been *cut off*.
   c. She *cut off* a big piece of meat and gave it to the dog.
4. a. Her health has really *picked up* since she moved to a sunny climate.
   b. Can you *pick up* my pen for me? It's under your chair.
   c. I *picked up* some Spanish when I was traveling in Peru.

Separable or inseparable?

3 These sentences all contain **separable** phrasal verbs. Replace the words in *italics* with a pronoun.
1. He turned on *the light*.   He turned it on.
2. She's taken off *her boots*.   She's taken them off.
3. He took up *golf* when he retired.
4. We picked up *Spanish* very quickly.
5. I looked up *the words* in my dictionary.
6. They brought up *five children* really well.
7. I've given up *sweets* at last.

4 These sentences all contain **inseparable** phrasal verbs. Replace the words in *italics* with a pronoun.
1. She takes after *her father*.   She takes after him.
2. Nearly everyone got through *the exam*.
3. We looked after *their cats*.
4. He gets along with *his sister*.
5. I'm looking for *my glasses*.
6. They're looking forward to *the vacation*.
7. We couldn't put up with *the noise* any longer.

Talking about you

5 Complete the phrasal verbs in the questions with **one** of the words in the box. Then ask and answer the questions with a partner.

| with | up | to | after |

1. Who do you take _____ in your family?
2. Do you get along _____ both your parents?
3. Have you recently taken _____ any new sports or hobbies?
4. Do you often look _____ words in your dictionary?
5. Are you looking forward _____ going on vacation soon?
6. Do you pick _____ foreign languages easily?
7. Do you have any bad habits that you want to give _____ ?

CD1 47 Listen and compare your answers.

EVERYDAY ENGLISH
Polite requests and offers

1 Match a line in **A** with a line in **B**. Who is talking to who? Where are the conversations taking place?

A	B
1. ___ I'll give you a ride into town, if you like.	a. Diet or regular?
2. ___ It's a present. Do you think you could gift wrap it for me?	b. Go ahead. It's very stuffy in here.
3. ___ Pump number 5. And could you give me a token for the car wash?	c. One moment. I'll have to look it up.
4. ___ Two large Cokes, please.	d. I'm sorry, it's not working today.
5. ___ Could you show me how you did that?	e. Oh, sorry, I didn't realize that you couldn't get through.
6. ___ Would you mind moving your car?	f. Yes, of course. I'll just take the tag off.
7. ___ Would you mind if I opened the window?	g. That would be great. Could you drop me at the library?
8. ___ Can you tell me the code for Tokyo, please?	h. Certainly. Just go to "System Preferences" and click on "Displays."

CD1 48 Listen and check your answers.

Music of English

English voice range is very wide, especially in polite requests.

1 **CD1 49** Listen and repeat.

Could you show me how you did that?
Would you mind moving your car?

2 **CD1 49** Listen again to the lines in Exercise 1. Practice the conversations.

▶▶ Grammar Reference 4.6–4.7 p. 134

2 **CD1 50** Listen to four more conversations. What is each one about?

1. _____ 3. _____
2. _____ 4. _____

3 Listen again. What are the exact words of the request or offer? Try to remember the conversations with your partner.

Role play

Work with a partner. Choose a situation and act it out in front of the class.

In a restaurant	In a clothing store	At home
Student A you are a vegetarian customer **Student B** you are a waiter	**Student A** you want to buy a sweater **Student B** you are the sales assistant	**Student A** you are having a party **Student B** you are a friend, offer to help
table by the window menu ready to order vegetarian eat fish dessert coffee the check	help sweater in the window only color try on – my size really suits on sale 70% discount bargain – take it	come over and help buy drinks, etc. on your way while preparing food decorate the room, blow up balloons set up the music system choose some CDs doorbell! – let the guests in

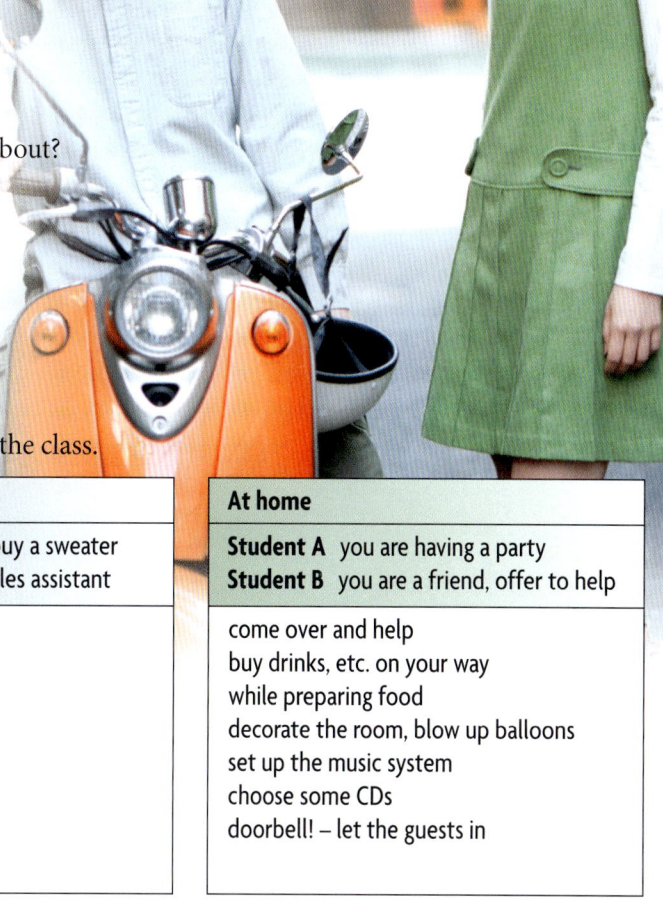

5 Our changing world

Grammar: Future forms • *may, might, could*
Vocabulary: Word building
Everyday English: Arranging to meet

STARTER Scientists predict that global warming will change our world forever. Look at the photos. What do you think will happen?

I think/don't think that ... will ...

THINGS OUR GRANDCHILDREN MAY NEVER SEE
Making predictions

1 **CD2 2** Hannah and Dan are expecting their first baby. They're looking at the photos in the newspaper. Listen to their conversation. Answer the questions.
   1. What is Hannah worried about?
   2. Why is Dan surprised?
   3. What do the scientists say about the future?
   4. What examples of global warming does Hannah mention?
   5. How does Dan try to reassure Hannah? What does he say?

2 Listen again and complete the lines with the *exact* words from the conversation.
   1. What _____ the world _____ like when he or she grows up?
   2. Don't they make you worry about what _____ happen in the future?
   3. Of course, things _____ change a lot in the next hundred years, …
   4. No one says it _____ get warmer or it _____ get warmer anymore.
   5. Scientists say that it definitely _____ warmer.
   6. They say temperatures _____ rise by up to 39°F.
   7. You _____ a baby soon.
   8. We _____ do our part.
   9. OK, but maybe it _____ help. It _____ too late already.

34 Unit 5 • Our changing world

What do you think will happen?

3 Work in groups. Ask questions about the future with *Do you think … will …?* Answer with *may, might, could,* or *will*.

1. the earth/continue to get warmer?

> Do you think the earth will continue to get warmer?
>
> Yes, it will, definitely.
>
> I'm not so sure. It might.
>
> I don't think it will.

2. all the ice/melt at the Poles?
3. polar bears/become extinct?
4. more people/travel by train?
5. air travel/banned to reduce CO₂ emissions?
6. new sources of energy/found?
7. there/be more droughts or floods in the world?
8. lifestyles/have to change?

CD2 3 Listen and compare your ideas.

PRACTICE

Discussing grammar

1 Work with a partner. Decide which is the correct verb form.

1. **A** Have you decided about your vacation yet?
   B No, not yet. We've never been to Costa Rica so we *will / might* go there.
2. **A** *Will you / Are you going to* take an umbrella?
   B No, I'm not. The forecast says it*'ll / might* be fine all day.
3. **A** Why are you making a list?
   B Because *I'll go / I'm going* shopping. Is there anything you want?
4. **A** Would you like to go out to dinner tonight?
   B Sorry, *I'll work / I'm working* late. How about tomorrow night? *I'll call / I'm calling* you.
5. **A** What *are you doing / will you do* Saturday night?
   B I'm not sure yet. I *will / may* go to a friend's or she *will / may* come here.
6. **A** Are you enjoying your job more now?
   B No, I'm not. *I'm going to / I will* look for another one.
7. **A** Your team's no good! It's 2–0 Brazil!
   B Come on. It's only half-time. I think they *are going to / could* still win.
8. **A** You *won't pass / aren't passing* your exams next month if you go out every night.
   B I know, *I might / I'll* study harder. I promise.

CD2 4 Listen and check. Practice the conversations, paying attention to stress and intonation.

GRAMMAR SPOT

1 Which predictions are most sure? Which are less sure?

   It **might/may/could** change.
   It **is going to/will** change.

2 Which *two* answers to the question are correct? Which is not? Why?

   "Can you come on Sunday?"

   Sorry, I can't. | I'm seeing / I'm going to see / I'll see | my grandmother.

3 Which of these future forms expresses …?
   • an intention • a prediction • an arrangement

   Our love **will last** forever.
   I'm going to start exercising next week.
   We're meeting James at 11:00 in the conference room.

▶▶ Grammar Reference 5.1–5.3 p. 135

Unit 5 • Our changing world   35

World weather warnings

2 What are these extreme types of weather?

thunderstorms   floods   hurricane   heatwave   snowstorms

3 **CD2 5** Listen to five short weather forecasts from around the world. Number the countries in the order you hear them.

The U.S. ☐	Thailand 1	Mexico ☐	South Africa ☐	Canada ☐

4 Listen again to the forecasts. Make notes about the weather in each country.

5 Work with a partner. Use your notes to describe the weather in each country. What's the weather forecast for where *you* are for the next few days?

I think/don't think . . .

6 Make sentences with *I think . . . will* and the prompts in **A**. Match them with a sentence in **B**.

I think it'll be a cold night tonight. Wear warm clothes if you go out.

A	B
1. it/a cold night tonight	__ But we'd better get moving.
2. I/get a new computer	1 Wear warm clothes if you go out.
3. I/take a cooking class	__ I want a laptop this time.
4. you/like the movie	__ You have all the right qualifications.
5. we/get to the airport in time	__ It's a great story and really well cast.
6. you/get the job	__ I can't even boil an egg.

CD2 6 Listen and check. Practice the lines.

7 Make sentences with *I don't think . . . will* and the words in **A** in Exercise 6. Match them with a sentence in **C**.

I don't think it'll be a cold night tonight. You won't need to take a jacket.

C
__ There's too much traffic.
__ I'll get lessons from my mom.
__ It may seem old-fashioned to you but it's OK for me.
1 You won't need to take a jacket.
__ You're too young and you have no experience.
__ It's not really your kind of thing.

CD2 7 Listen and check. Practice the lines and continue some of them.

Talking about you

8 Make true sentences about *you*. Say them aloud in small groups.

1. I/go for coffee after class
2. I/go shopping this afternoon
3. I/eat out tonight
4. our teacher/tell us that our English/improving
5. it/rain tomorrow
6. my grandchildren/go on vacation on the moon

I might go for a coffee.

I think/don't think I'll go for coffee.

36 Unit 5 • Our changing world

LISTENING AND SPEAKING
Rocket man

1 Look at the pictures. Which rockets do you recognize?

2 Read about Steve Bennett. Who is he? What was his dream? How is it coming true? What do you understand by *space tourism*?

Rocket Man
Steve Bennett

As a little boy, like lots of little boys, Steve Bennett dreamed of becoming a spaceman, but unlike most little boys, Steve's dream is coming true. Steve is a leading rocket scientist and he's now building his own rocket. In a few years he's going to travel into space with two other passengers. He believes the age of mass space tourism is on the horizon.

3 **CD2 8** Steve was interviewed for a radio program called *Saturday Live*. Close your books. Listen to the interview.
- What's your impression of Steve? Would you describe him as "a realist" or "a dreamer"? Professional or amateur?
- Would you like to travel with him into space?

4 Work with a partner. Read the questions below. Which can you answer?
1. Why is Steve so sure space tourism will happen? Why are Richard Branson and Jeff Bezos called "big names"?
2. In what way does he compare space travel with the Internet?
3. How will the passengers be like the early American astronauts? What are they *not* going to do?
4. What influenced Steve as a small child? Why is his rocket called *Thunderstar*? What was he not allowed to watch?
5. What was his parents' attitude about space travel?
6. Why does he think it is necessary for humans to be in space?
7. Why is skydiving good training for space tourists?
8. How much has the couple paid?
9. What does Steve think about every day?

CD2 8 Listen again and check your ideas.

What do you think?
- Is space tourism a good idea?
- Is space travel important to the world? Why/Why not?
- Should the money be spent on other things? Give examples.

SPOKEN ENGLISH *pretty*

1 Look at how Steve uses *pretty* in the interview.
   I kept it **pretty** quiet ...
   That's **pretty** much where the human race needs to be.

2 The adverb *pretty* is often used in informal, spoken English. It means "not a lot" but "more than a little."
   She's **pretty** nice.
   The weather was **pretty** bad.

3 Work with a partner. Ask the questions and reply including *pretty* in the answer.
   1. A Did your team win?
      B No, but they did well.
   2. A You haven't lost your cell phone again!
      B No, no. I'm sure it's in my bag somewhere.
   3. A Do you enjoy skiing?
      B I do, but I'm hopeless at it.
   4. A What do you think of my English?
      B I think it's good.

   CD2 9 Listen and check. Practice again.

▶▶ WRITING WRITING FOR TALKING **CD2 10** *p. 103*

Unit 5 • Our changing world   37

READING AND SPEAKING
Life fifty years from now

1. The future is difficult to predict. What things in our lives today do you think scientists fifty years ago did NOT predict?

2. Look at the text "Life in 2060." Read the introduction and paragraph headings 1–7 only. What do *you* predict about the topics?

3. Which sentences a–g do you think go with which topic?

   a. Lost limbs will regrow, hearts will regenerate.
   b. This knowledge will help reduce suicide rates, one of the major causes of death worldwide.
   c. ... the most sensational discovery ever, that is, confirmation that life really does exist on Mars.
   d. It is now routine to extend the lives of laboratory animals by 40%.
   e. ... your fridge will "know" when you are low on milk or any other item, ...
   f. Soon their existence will be no more controversial than the existence of other galaxies 100 years ago.
   g. It could cause a global revulsion against eating meat ...

4. Read the article and put sentences a–g in the right place.

5. Are these statements true (✓) or false (✗)?

   1. Women will be able to give birth at the age of 100.
   2. It will be possible to replace all the parts of the body.
   3. Animal parts will be used for human organ transplants.
   4. Scientists think that computers won't ever do the work of the human brain.
   5. Scientists believe that if we can talk to animals, we won't want to eat them.
   6. Alien life has already been found on Mars.
   7. There could be an infinite number of other universes.
   8. The walls in your house will change color to suit your mood.
   9. Your armchair will help you do your housework.
   10. Pills will replace food.

What do you think?

- Read the article again and <u>underline</u> the predictions that most surprise you.
  Which do you believe will definitely happen?
  Which might happen?
  Which do you believe won't happen?
- What predictions can you make? Choose from these topics:

transportation	jobs	television	communication
the home	food	clothes	sports

38 Unit 5 • Our changing world

Life in

An international group of forty scientists have made some very surprising predictions about the future. They say that in the next fifty years the way we live will change beyond our wildest dreams. Here are some of their predictions. You may find some of them surprising.
BEA ROSENTHAL reports.

1 Life expectancy
Within 50 years, living to 100 while still enjoying active, healthy lives will be the norm. Professor Richard Miller of the University of Michigan says: " ⬜ We will be able to do the same for humans." So with regular injections, centenarians will be as vigorous as today's sixty-year-olds. Women will be able to give birth well into old age; their biological clocks could be extended by ten years.

2 Growing body parts
Professor Ellen Heber-Katz says: "People will take for granted that injured or diseased organs can be repaired in much the same way as we fix a car. ⬜ Damaged parts will be replaced. Within 50 years whole-body replacement will be routine." But doctors will need huge supplies of organs for transplant. Where will they come from? Scientists say these could be grown inside animals from human cells.

3 Understanding the brain
We don't yet know how the brain gives us our awareness of being alive. "But," says Professor Susan Greenfield of Oxford University, "in 50 years we may have a clearer idea of how the brain generates consciousness." Studies of the brain and the nature of consciousness will bring much greater understanding of disorders such as schizophrenia and depression. ⬜ Other scientists go further than Professor Greenfield. They believe that by 2060 computers will develop their own consciousness and emotions. Human beings may eventually be replaced by computers in some areas of life.

2060

4 Understanding animals

Thanks to a device which can "read" emotions, feelings, and thoughts, we will be able to "talk" to animals. The story of Dr. Dolittle* will be fact, not fiction. "This could first work with primates, then mammals, then other vertebrates, including fish," says Professor Daniel Pauly from Canada. "_____, so we might all become vegetarian."

* fictional character for children

5 Discovering aliens

A number of scientists predict that the biggest breakthrough in the next 50 years will be the discovery of extraterrestrial beings. Dr. Chris McKay of NASA says: "We may find evidence of alien life frozen in the ancient permafrost on Mars." Scientists hope that the current interest in space missions to this planet means that there is every chance of making _____ Dr. McKay also believes that evidence of alien life forms may even be found here on Earth.

6 Parallel universes

Advances in quantum physics will prove that there are parallel universes. In fact there may be an infinite number of them. These universes will contain space, time, and some of them may even contain you in a slightly different form. For years parallel universes only existed in the works of science fiction, but now Professor Max Tegmark says: "_____."

7 Our homes

What might our houses be like in the second half of the 21st century? This is Professor Greenfield's prediction:

As you enter the living room, sensors will detect your presence and the walls will start to glow. Talk to the walls and, activated by your voice, they will change to a color of your choice, "pink" to "green" to "blue," whatever suits your mood.

Sink into your glowing cyber-armchair, relax in the knowledge that the house computer will perform all your everyday household tasks. The voice system in the chair will address you by name and advise a change in position that will be better for your spine.

In the kitchen, _____ and it will automatically send orders to the supermarket. However, it is in the kitchen where "new" meets "old." Food remains in its old-fashioned form. Pills, so confidently predicted in the 20th-century to replace food, exist, but nobody wants them. There is too much pleasure in cooking, chewing, and tasting all kinds of food.

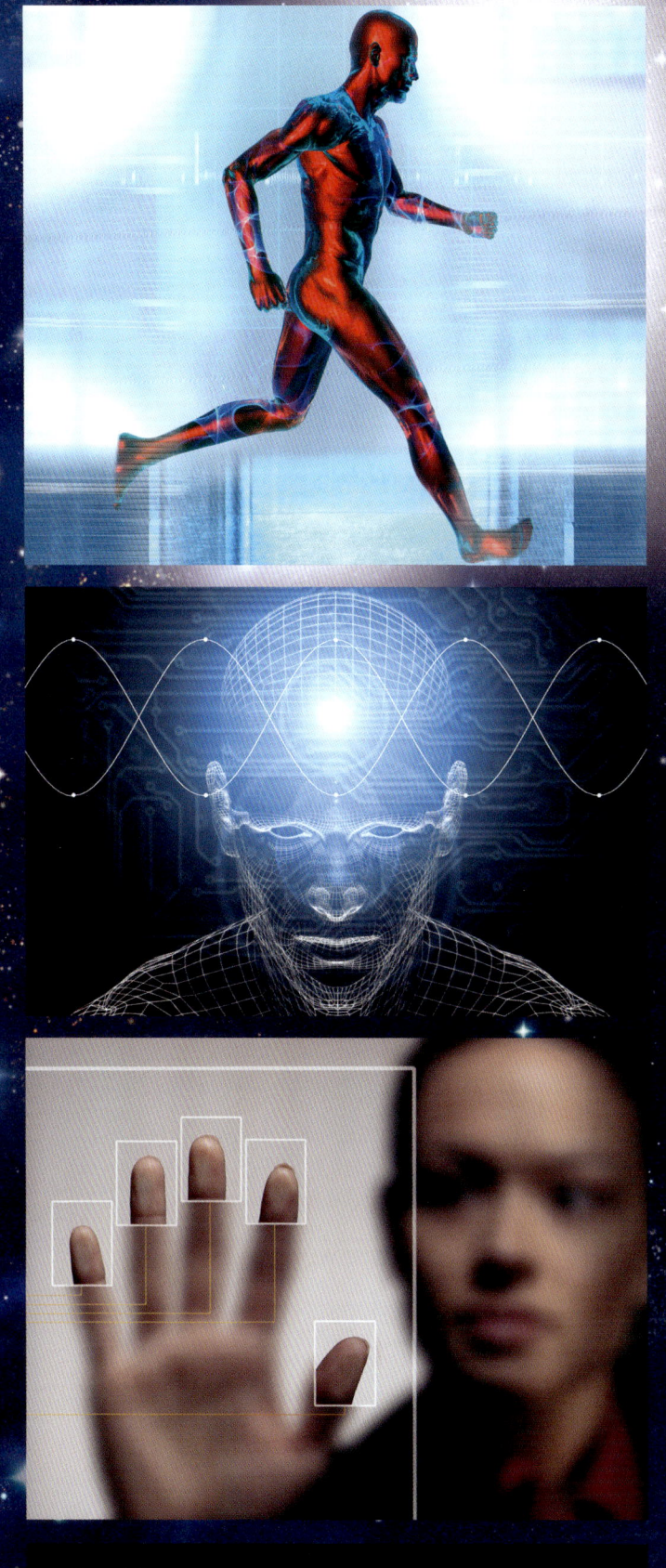

Finally

Predicting the future has occupied mankind for generations. However predictions have not always been correct. The huge influence of many of today's technical marvels, such as the Internet or cell phones, was never predicted.

VOCABULARY AND PRONUNCIATION
Word building – suffixes and prefixes

1 Work with a partner. Look at the information on suffixes.

> **SUFFIXES** are used to form different parts of speech. What endings do you notice on these words? What part of speech are they?
> act   ac**tion**   ac**tive**   active**ly**

What part of speech are the words in the box? What are the different word endings?

prediction	colorful	excitement	suitable
shorten	confidently	creative	business
automatically	imagination	qualify	careless

2 Look at the information on prefixes.

> **PREFIXES** are used to change the meaning of words. Look at these words with prefixes.
> **pre**dict   **re**grow   **extra**terrestrial   **dis**order
> Which means . . . ?
> before   outside   again
> Which is a negative prefix?

Choose a prefix from the box to make the words mean the opposite.

un-   in-   im-   il-   dis-   ir-

1. possible   *impossible*
2. patient
3. lucky
4. legal
5. appear
6. regular
7. formal
8. conscious

3 Work in two groups. Make new words with the base words using the suffixes and/or the prefixes. Which group can make the most words?

PREFIX	BASE WORD	SUFFIX
un-	agree	-ness
	arrange	
	conscious	
im- re-	expense	-ment -ion
	happy	
dis-	help	-ful
	kind	
	polite	-less -able
mis- in-	react	
	success	-ive
	understand	
	use	

4 Complete the sentences with a word from Exercise 3.
1. Carlos and Diana don't get along at all. They dis_____ about everything.
2. Money does not always lead to h_____ness.
3. My aunt says today's kids are all rude and im_____.
4. Thanks for your advice, it was really h_____ful. I really appreciate your k_____ness.
5. My dad is u_____less at fixing his computer. I always have to help him.
6. Please don't mis_____ me. I didn't mean to be un_____. I'm really sorry.
7. Timmy fell off his bike and hit his head. He was un_____ for a few hours.
8. What was your wife's re_____ion when she heard you'd won the lottery?

CD2 11 Listen and check.

Changing word stress

5 In some words the stressed syllable changes in the different forms. Read aloud these pairs of words.

'athlete ath'letic	pre'fer 'preference
i'magine imagi'nation	em'ployer emplo'yee

CD2 12 Listen and check. Practice again.

6 CD2 13 Listen to four short conversations. Write down the pairs of words with stress changes. Practice the conversations.

1. _____   _____
2. _____   _____
3. _____   _____
4. _____   _____

40   Unit 5 • Our changing world

EVERYDAY ENGLISH
Arranging to meet

1 **CD2 14** Listen to two friends, Gary and Mike, arranging to meet over the weekend. Complete the calendars.

Gary

22 FRIDAY
Morning
Afternoon
Evening

23 SATURDAY
Morning
Afternoon
Evening

24 SUNDAY
Morning

Mike

22 Friday
Morning
Afternoon — finish work early
Evening

23 Saturday
Morning
Afternoon
Evening

24 Sunday
Morning

Why is it difficult to find a time? Where and when do they finally agree to meet?

Making suggestions

2 **CD2 14** Listen again to the conversation. Complete the suggestions with the exact words Gary and Mike say.

1. I was _____ if we _____ meet.
2. I _____ meet you in the afternoon.
3. What _____ Saturday afternoon?
4. Is Saturday evening _____?
5. Why _____ we meet at the station?
6. _____ meet there for breakfast.
7. _____ about ten o'clock?
8. Can you _____ it 10:30?

Music of English 🎵

1 **CD2 15** Listen and repeat the suggestions in Exercise 2. Pay attention to the stress and intonation.

2 Work with a partner. Take turns reading aloud the suggestions and answering with a suitable reply from below.

> I'd love to – but …
> I'm afraid that's no good …
> Um, let me see.
> I can't, I have an appointment with …
> Sorry, the evening's out for me.
> Sounds good to me.
> Fine. 10:30 it is.

Role play

3 It is Saturday morning. You want to meet a friend over the weekend. Fill in your calendar. What are you doing this weekend? When are you free?

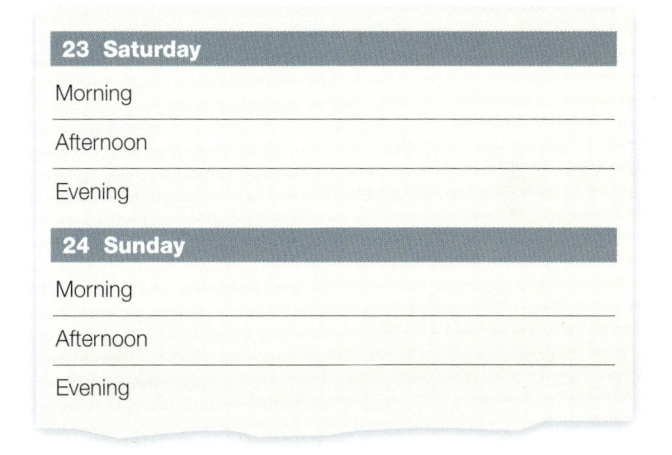

23 Saturday
Morning
Afternoon
Evening

24 Sunday
Morning
Afternoon
Evening

4 Find a partner. Make suggestions and arrange to meet.

> Are you doing anything on Saturday morning?
>
> I'm afraid I'm going …
>
> What about the afternoon?
>
> Let me see …
>
> I was wondering if you'd like to …

When you have finished, tell the class when and where you're meeting.

We're meeting on Saturday afternoon. We're going …

Unit 5 • Our changing world   41

6 What matters to me

Grammar: Information questions
Vocabulary: Adjectives and adverbs
Everyday English: In a department store

STARTER 1 Think of someone in the room. Don't say who it is.
The other students must ask questions to find out who it is.

*Is it a male or a female?   What color is her hair?
Does she have blue eyes?   What kind of clothes does she wear?*

2 Do the same about someone famous.

DESCRIPTIONS
Information questions

1 Match a question with an answer.

DESCRIBING PEOPLE	
1. _e_ What's she like?	a. She's in her twenties.
2. ___ What does she look like?	b. She likes snowboarding.
3. ___ What does she like doing?	c. Five foot eight.
4. ___ How tall is she?	d. She's tall and pretty.
5. ___ What color are her eyes?	e. She's really nice. Very easygoing.
6. ___ How old is she?	f. She's fine.
7. ___ What kind of clothes does she wear?	g. Blue.
8. ___ What's her hair like?	h. It's sort of long, blond, and straight.
9. ___ How is she?	i. Not formal. Casual. She has a lot of style.

CD2 16 Listen and check. Work with a partner. Practice the questions and answers. Cover one column, then the other.

2 Ask and answer the questions about a relative.

What's your brother like?

He's a great guy, very kind. You'd like him.

You can use the ideas in the box to help.

a lot of fun	a bit quiet	very sociable	good-looking
pretty dark	attractive	medium height	about six feet
in his mid-twenties	straight	short	curly

42 Unit 6 • What matters to me

3 <u>Underline</u> the correct answer.

DESCRIBING PLACES

1. What's your apartment like?
   It's modern, but it's cozy. / I like it.
2. How big is it?
   Yes, it is pretty big. / About 850 square feet.
3. How many rooms are there?
   There's a lot of room. / There are three rooms.
4. What size is the kitchen?
   It's square. / Nine feet by eight.
5. Which floor is it on?
   Wooden. / The fourth.
6. Which part of town is it in?
   It's south of the river. / I get the number 79 bus.
7. How far is it to the stores?
   Just five minutes. / It takes half an hour.

CD2 17 Listen and check. With your partner, practice the questions and answers.

4 Ask and answer questions about where you live. You can use the ideas in the box to help.

| on an old block | noisy | has a view of . . . |
| a terrace where we can sit outside |
| first floor | enormous | tiny |

What's your apartment like?

It's a bit small, but it's comfortable.

5 Look at the questions for describing things. Put a word from the box into each question.

| much | How | brand | of | long | for | size |

DESCRIBING THINGS

1. What _____ is it? *Sony.*
2. How _____ does it weigh? *3 pounds.*
3. What's it made _____? *Carbon and titanium.*
4. What's this button _____? *It turns it on.*
5. _____ big is the screen? *13.2 inches.*
6. How _____ is the battery life? *Eight hours.*
7. What _____ is the hard disk? *80 gigabytes.*

CD2 18 Listen and check. With your partner, practice the questions and answers.

6 Ask and answer similar questions about your laptop/cell phone/camera/MP3 player.

What brand is it?

It's a Dell.

GRAMMAR SPOT

1 *What* and *which* can be followed by a noun.
   What color/**Which** floor . . . ?
   Find examples on these pages.

2 *How* can be followed by an adjective or an adverb.
   How tall/far . . . ?
   Find examples.

3 Match a question and an answer.

   | What's she like? | Very well, thanks. |
   | How is she? | Very nice and pretty. |

▶▶ Grammar Reference 6.1–6.2 p. 136

PRACTICE

Getting information

Ask questions for these situations.

1. Do you have whole wheat bread? White bread?
   What kind of bread do you have?
2. Would you like vanilla ice cream? Strawberry? Chocolate?
3. Do we go left or right at the traffic lights? Or straight?
4. Is your camera a Canon? A Samsung? An Olympus?
5. Do you like pasta? Hamburgers? Spicy food?
6. Is that your sister's top you're wearing? Suzie's? Or your own?
7. Does it take 30 minutes to get to the airport? An hour?
8. Is your house half a mile from the beach? One mile?
9. Do you go to the movies once a week? Every other day?
10. Do two of you want coffee? Four of you? All of you?
11. Do you wear size eight shoes? Nine? Ten?

CD2 19 Listen and compare.

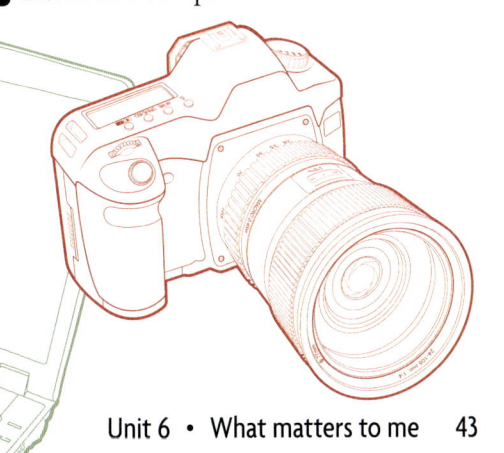

Unit 6 • What matters to me   43

VOCABULARY
Adjectives

1 Work in pairs. Look at advertisements 1–3. Which advertisement is for …?

a date   something to eat   a vacation destination

2 Find some adjectives in the ads.

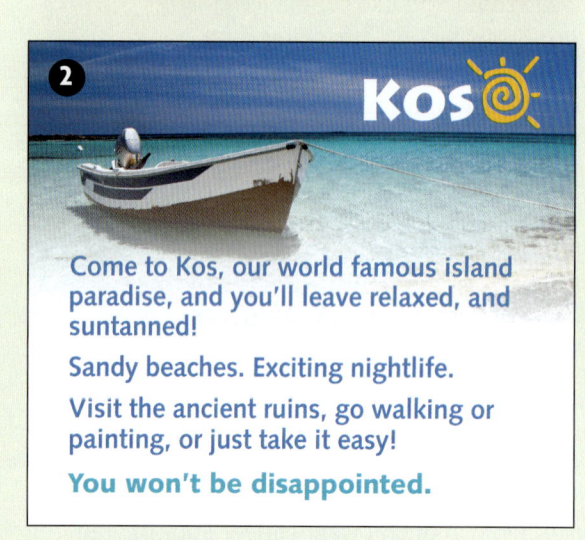

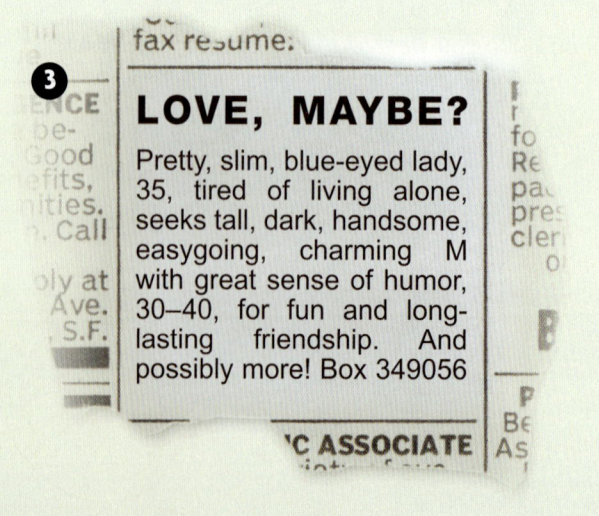

1

Mamma Mia

Mamma Mia pasta sauces. From much-loved Bolognese to our latest garlic and basil. Made from the finest organic ingredients in the old-fashioned way.

So tempting!
Just like homemade.
You'll be amazed!

2 Kos

Come to Kos, our world famous island paradise, and you'll leave relaxed, and suntanned!

Sandy beaches. Exciting nightlife.

Visit the ancient ruins, go walking or painting, or just take it easy!

You won't be disappointed.

3 LOVE, MAYBE?

Pretty, slim, blue-eyed lady, 35, tired of living alone, seeks tall, dark, handsome, easygoing, charming M with great sense of humor, 30–40, for fun and long-lasting friendship. And possibly more! Box 349056

-ed and -ing adjectives

3 How do these words end in the advertisements?

amaz-   relax-   excit-   disappoint-   tir-   charm-

Complete the sentences with one of these adjectives ending in -ed or -ing.

1. Having a massage is very _relaxing_ .
2. I was _____ when they offered me the job. I was sure I'd blown the interview.
3. Our vacation was _____ . It rained every day.
4. I was so _____ on my wedding day, I couldn't eat.
5. The trip was very _____ . I was exhausted.
6. He says such nice things. He is _____ . He makes you feel so special.

Adjectives and nouns that go together

4 Some adjectives and nouns often go together.

sandy beach   ancient ruins

Match an adjective and a noun. Sometimes there is more than one possibility.

adjective	noun
fresh latest pretty clear fast crowded casual close handsome straight cozy challenging	friend fruit clothes fashions hair job restaurant food woman man room sky

CD2 20 Listen and check.

Compound adjectives

5 Find some compound adjectives in the ads.

much-loved   old-fashioned

Match a word from **A** and **B** to make compound adjectives.

A	B
well (×2) full long good second eye brand	new dressed hand behaved time looking catching term

Think of a noun that goes with each adjective. What's the opposite?

full-time job   part-time job

6 Test each other on the compound adjectives in Exercise 5.

> Another word for handsome.
> good-looking

> What kind of job is it if you work forty hours a week?
> full-time

44 Unit 6 • What matters to me

Adverbs

1 Look at advertisements 4–6. Which ad is for …?
a pain killer   a watch   a house to rent

2 Find adverbs that end in *-ly* in advertisements 4 and 5.
simply   beautifully

Find some adverbs that don't end in *-ly* in advertisement 6.
just   too

4

LOG FIRES IN THE CATSKILLS

$1,250 pw

Live simply in this beautifully restored 19th century country cottage. Sit peacefully in front of the fire. Situated in a charming town, sleeps 6, fully equipped.

andycurran@fastnetus.com

5 You don't actually own one of our handmade instruments. You merely look after it for the next generation.

Probably the best investment you'll ever make.

6 Painful headaches that just won't go? Backache, too?

Relieve aches and pains fast with Cuprodil! Cuprodil goes straight to the pain.

You'll soon feel good again!

✨ **CUPRODIL**

Adverbs and verbs that go together

3 Some verbs and adverbs often go together.
drive carefully   walk slowly   explain clearly

Match a verb and an adverb. Sometimes there is more than one possibility.

verb	abverb
wait sit behave	badly peacefully heavily
shine fight leave	quickly patiently fluently
whisper die rain	suddenly deeply brightly
act speak breathe	comfortably softly bravely

4 Act out some of the verbs and adverbs in front of the class.

You're driving carefully!   *You're waiting patiently!*

Adverbs that don't end in *-ly*

5 Complete the sentences with an adverb from the box.

again	fast	hard	loud	wrong
even	right	straight	together	almost

1. Peter and I lived _____ in college.
2. He's a good student. He tries _____ .
3. "Where's the town hall?" "Go _____ ahead."
4. Say that _____ . I didn't hear you.
5. Don't talk so _____ ! Everyone can hear you.
6. Why do you drive so _____ ? Slow down!
7. His wife's name is Mariana, not Maria! Get it _____ .
8. The vacation was a disaster. Everything went _____ .
9. This room is cool, _____ in summer.
10. "Are you ready?" "_____ . Give me another five minutes."

CD2 21 Listen and check.

Project – My most treasured possession

1 **CD2 22** Listen to three people describing what they'd save if their home was on fire. What is it? Why would they save it?

2 What is *your* most treasured possession? Prepare to talk about it.

I couldn't live without my . . .
It's important to me because . . .
It was given to me by . . .
I've had it for . . .
It reminds me of . . .

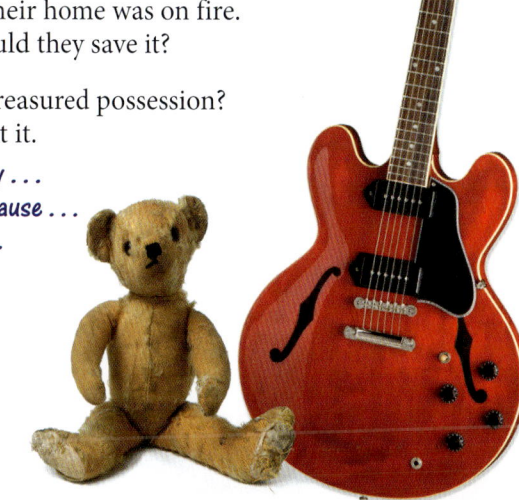

READING AND SPEAKING
The heart of the home

1. Close your eyes and think of your kitchen at home.
   - Who's in it?
   - What's happening?
   - What are they doing?
   - What can you smell?

2. Read the introduction to **My Kitchen** at the top of page 47. Do you agree that the kitchen is the heart of the home? Is it where *your* family gets together?

3. Work in three groups.

   Group A Read about **Santina**, from Italy.
   Group B Read about **Elizabeth**, from the United States.
   Group C Read about **Lakshmamma**, from India.

   Answer the questions.
   1. What does she do?
   2. What does her husband do?
   3. Where does she live?
   4. What's her house like?
   5. How does she feel about her kitchen?
   6. Is her life easy or difficult?
   7. What does her family eat?
   8. Does she seem to be happy?
   9. What do you think she worries about?

4. Find a partner from the other groups. Compare and swap information.

5. Which person is most likely to say …?
   1. *"I can never decide where to go swimming."*
   2. *"We have found you a very nice girl. Why won't you marry her?"*
   3. *"If anyone wants me, I'm weeding and watering."*
   4. *"I'm too busy to cook today."*
   5. *"I live my life in tune with nature."*
   6. *"I'd love to have a new kitchen."*

What do you think?

In your opinion, who …?
- is the wealthiest materially
- is the happiest spiritually
- is the most creative cook
- has the hardest life

Give reasons for your answers.

Speaking

1. What food do you most associate with home? Is there a particular day of the week or time of year when you eat it?
2. Talk about your kitchen. Answer questions 1–12 from the text.

▶▶ **WRITING** DESCRIBING A PLACE *p. 104*

46 Unit 6 • What matters to me

My Kitchen

Italy

Homemaker Santina Corvaglia, 61, lives in an old two bedroom farmhouse in southeast Italy with her husband, Carlo, 56, who's a mechanic. They have a 31-year-old daughter, Francesca.

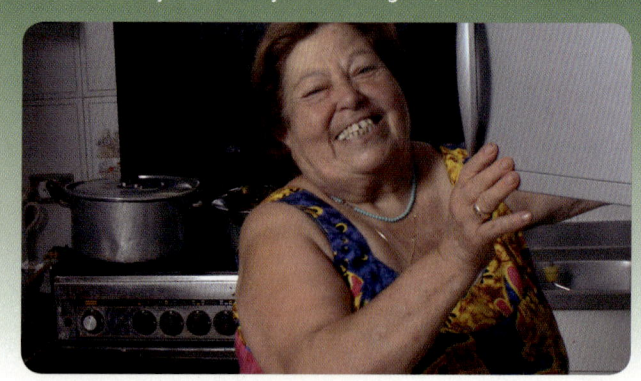

1. **Q** How much is your house worth?
   A About $80,000.

2. **Q** What is your kitchen like?
   A It's not very big. It's my little corner of the house. It's where I belong, and where I'm happiest.

3. **Q** How big is it?
   A 129 sq. ft.

4. **Q** What's your favorite thing?
   A My cabinets full of different Italian herbs.

5. **Q** How much time do you spend in the kitchen?
   A About four hours every day. And the same in the garden.

6. **Q** How many meals do you cook a day?
   A Three. For the three of us, and whoever comes by—friends, relatives. My family is the most important thing to me. I want grandchildren!

7. **Q** What's in your fridge and cabinets?
   A Vegetables, water, milk, eggs, cheese, ham, sausages, lemonade, butter, pasta, canned tomatoes, beans, honey, and homemade jam.

8. **Q** What would make your life easier in the kitchen?
   A Nothing. I have all I need.

9. **Q** Who helps you?
   A My daughter helps sometimes. My husband wouldn't dream of it, and I wouldn't want him to.

10. **Q** How often do you sit down and eat together as a family?
    A Twice a day.

11. **Q** How much do you spend on groceries every week?
    A I grow my own vegetables, and we have chickens and rabbits, so I only spend about $50 a week. But there is a drought this year.

12. **Q** What can you see from your kitchen windows?
    A My garden, my orchard, and my olive trees.

The kitchen is the **heart of the home**. It's where the family gets together for the important things in life—food, conversation, and celebration. Three women from around the world invite us into their kitchens. PENNY ROGERS reports.

California, U.S.

Elizabeth Anne Hogan, 45, is a lifestyle coach living in a 16-room house on the beach in California. It has six bathrooms, five bedrooms, and a swimming pool. Her husband, Mike, 47, is a businessman. They have two children: Hailey, 14, and Hanna, 9.

1. **Q** How much is your house worth?
   A About $800,000.
2. **Q** What is your kitchen like?
   A The kitchen is futuristic. I don't know how everything works, so it's all a bit "alien" to me.
3. **Q** How big is it?
   A 200 sq. ft.
4. **Q** What's your favorite thing?
   A The two ovens, but they take up too much space.
5. **Q** How much time do you spend in the kitchen?
   A About seven to eight hours a day. But not cooking. It's the room we live in.
6. **Q** How many meals do you cook a day?
   A Two to three, if you count cereal and bagels. But only one, if you mean actually doing things with real food.
7. **Q** What's in your fridge and cabinets?
   A Fruit, vegetables, chips, milk, yogurt, takeout, cheeses, and cereal. A lot of takeout food. And dog food.
8. **Q** What would make your life easier in the kitchen?
   A A chef. We do everything for the kids ourselves. No nannies, housekeepers, or cooks for them.
9. **Q** Who helps you?
   A My husband and kids take food out of takeout containers and put it on plates. Does that count as helping?
10. **Q** How often do you sit down and eat together as a family?
    A Every morning and evening.
11. **Q** How much do you spend on groceries every week?
    A $200. Everything is low-fat and organic, pre-packed and prepared. It's all delivered.
12. **Q** What can you see from your kitchen windows?
    A A panoramic, 180-degree view of the Pacific Ocean.

India

Lakshmamma, 50, is a homemaker living in a three-roomed mud hut near Bangalore. Her husband, Adaviyappa, 55, works on a cattle farm. They have two sons, Gangaraju, 30, and Ravi, 25, who both live at home.

1. **Q** How much is your house worth?
   A To rebuild it would cost about $2,000.
2. **Q** What is your kitchen like?
   A It's small and dark. I dislike just about everything about it. It's so old.
3. **Q** How big is it?
   A 54 sq. ft.
4. **Q** What's your favorite thing?
   A The stone where I grind my spices.
5. **Q** How much time do you spend in the kitchen?
   A Six to seven hours a day—sometimes more. I'm always cooking or washing.
6. **Q** How many meals do you cook a day?
   A Two or three.
7. **Q** What's in your fridge and cabinets?
   A We don't have a fridge. On shelves I have lentils, rice, spices such as chilies, turmeric powder, some vegetables, and salt.
8. **Q** What would make your life easier in the kitchen?
   A Running water. A daughter-in-law would be good as well! But God has given me life and I am grateful.
9. **Q** Who helps you?
   A My sons help when they have time. My husband doesn't help.
10. **Q** How often do you sit down and eat together as a family?
    A Men eat before women in our community. We don't eat together.
11. **Q** How much do you spend on groceries every week?
    A $15. Sometimes less. It depends how much money we have.
12. **Q** What can you see from your kitchen windows?
    A Not much! I have no windows in my kitchen.

LISTENING AND SPEAKING
My closest relative

1. Discuss the statements in small groups. Are they true for your family?
   - Mothers feel closer to their sons.
     Fathers feel closer to their daughters.
   - The first-born child is ambitious, responsible, dominant, and insecure.
     The second child is free, independent, creative, and easygoing.
     The last-born child is the baby—spoiled, happy, confident, and secure.

2. **CD2 23** Listen to five people talking about who they feel closest to in their family. Complete the chart.

	Jen	Brett	Julia	Susan	Chris
I feel closest to …	my mother				
He/she is easy to talk to.	✓				
We do things together.					
We have a similar character.					
I like the way he/she thinks.					
We are different.					

3. Who said these expressions? What do you understand by them?
   1. *"We have our ups and downs, of course …"*
   2. *"We don't really see eye to eye on anything."*
   3. *"In many ways she drives me crazy."*
   4. *"We're like oil and water."*
   5. *"They fight like cats and dogs."*

SPOKEN ENGLISH Adding emphasis

1. We can change the order of words in a sentence to add emphasis. What is the more usual word order for these sentences?
   1. *She's very open, my mother.*
   2. *My father I don't really get along with.*
   3. *My mother I hardly ever see.*
   4. *He's pretty cool, my dad.*
   5. *Me, I'm a lot quieter.*

2. Notice how these sentences add emphasis.

   What I like about her is her attitude.
   What I like about him is that he's interesting and interested.
   The thing I love about her is the way everyone knows her.

3. What could people say about …?
   1. Joe: his sense of humor
             the way he makes everyone laugh
   2. Tina: her kindness
             the way she makes everyone feel good
   3. Beth: her attitude to life
             the fact she doesn't care what other people think

Discussion

- Work in pairs. Discuss who you feel closest to in your family, and why.
- Work in groups of four. Who has a similar family relationship to yours?
- Discuss as a class. Which family member are most people closest to?

EVERYDAY ENGLISH
In a department store

1. What are the big department stores in your town? What are they famous for? Do you like shopping in them?

2. Look at the board showing where the various departments are in a store.

   Where would you find …?
   - a tie
     in menswear, on the first floor
   - a wallet
   - earrings
   - a saucepan
   - a hairdryer
   - shower gel
   - a doll
   - a DVD player
   - women's boots
   - the ladies' room
   - a birthday card
   - a shaving mirror
   - lipstick
   - a vase
   - sneakers
   - a sofa
   - sheets
   - a suitcase
   - a pair of tights
   - a light snack

Store Guide

4 Fourth Floor
Toys and Babywear
Hair Salon
TV, Audio, and Phones
Sports

3 Third Floor
Furniture
Linens
Bathroom Accessories
The Terrace Cafeteria
Restrooms
Baby Facilities

2 Second Floor
Ladies' Fashions
Lingerie
Leather goods
Luggage

1 First Floor
Menswear
Stationery
Toiletries
Jewelry
Cosmetics

B Basement
Kitchenware
China and Glassware
Electrical Appliances

3. In which department could you see these signs?

   a. Cut and blow dry $50 / Highlights from $70
   b. Buy two coffee mugs, get one free!
   c. Travel in style— matching bags for long weekend breaks or short vacations
   d. Half price! Final clearance on men's sweaters before the spring!
   e. CUSTOMERS ARE REMINDED THAT ONLY FOOD AND DRINK PURCHASED ON THESE PREMISES MAY BE CONSUMED HERE
   f. Back to school! Beat the rush. Get your pens, paper, and folders NOW!

4. Which of these two signs …?
   - is telling you how to take things back
   - is inviting you to save as you spend

   Open a loyalty card today and you will receive a 10% discount on all your purchases.

   If goods are returned in their original packaging with a receipt within 28 days we will offer an exchange or refund.

5. **CD2 24** Listen to some conversations in a department store. Which department are they in? What are they trying to buy?

6. Listen again and complete the lines.

   1. A _____ do you wear?
      B Nine. That's 41, isn't it?
      A _____ 43 would be more comfortable, sir.

   2. B I'm afraid _____. We're _____ that size.
      A Will you _____ any more _____?
      B We should _____ by the end of the week.

   3. A Do you have _____?
      B No, we don't. They all _____.

   4. A Would you like me _____?
      B Ooh, _____! Thank you so much!

   5. A It _____. It's too tight.
      B Too bad. It _____. What _____ of?
      A Cashmere. It's so soft!

   6. A Keep your _____. That's your warranty.
      B _____ is the _____ for?
      A For a year.

   With a partner, practice the conversations.

7. Practice having conversations in other departments. Act them out in front of the class.

Unit 6 • What matters to me   49

Writing

UNIT 1	**AN INFORMAL LETTER** p. 99		Finding and correcting language mistakes in an informal letter
UNIT 2	**LETTERS AND E-MAILS** p. 100		Formal and informal language, beginnings and endings
UNIT 3	**TELLING A STORY (1)** p. 101		Linking ideas in a narrative
UNIT 4	**A BIOGRAPHY** p. 102		Combining sentences to avoid repetition
UNIT 5	**WRITING FOR TALKING** p. 103		Planning and writing a talk
UNIT 6	**DESCRIBING A PLACE** p. 104		Describing a room using relative pronouns and participles

REFERENCE

Audio Scripts p. 114

Grammar Reference p. 129

Extra Materials p. 143

Word Lists p. 148

Verb Patterns p. 154

Irregular Verbs and Phonetic Symbols p. 155

UNIT 1 AN INFORMAL LETTER – Correcting mistakes (1)

1. It is important to try to correct your own mistakes when you write. Look at the symbols in the box. What kind of mistakes do they signify?

2. Read the letter that Valeria, a student from Argentina, has written to her Canadian friend, Stephanie. Use the symbols to help you correct her mistakes.

T Tense	WW Wrong word
Prep Preposition	P Punctuation
Gr Grammar	Sp Spelling
WO Word order	λ Word missing

23 St. Mary's Road,
Philadelphia, PA
Tuesday, May 10

Dear Stephanie,

How are you? I'm very well. I came <u>in</u> [Prep] Philadelphia two weeks ago <u>for to</u> [Gr] study at a language school. I want λ learn <u>english</u> [Gr] because λ is a very important language. I'm <u>stay</u> [Gr] with λ [Gr] <u>a</u> American family. They have two <u>son</u> [Gr] and a <u>dauhgter</u> [Sp]. Mr. Kendall is λ teacher and Mrs. Kendall wor<u>k</u> [Gr] in a hospital. The Americans <u>is</u> [Gr] very kind, but they speak very quickly!

I study in the morning. My teacher<u>s</u> [P] name is Ann. She <u>said</u> [WW] me that my English is OK, but I <u>do</u> [WW] a lot of mistakes. Ann <u>don't</u> [Gr] give us too much homework, so in the afternoons I <u>go always</u> [WO] sightseeing. Philadelphia is much <u>more big</u> [Gr] than my town. I like <u>very much art</u> [WO] and I'm very interest<u>ing</u> [Gr] <u>for</u> [Prep] history, so I visit monuments and museums. I met a girl named Carla. She <u>came</u> [T] from Mexico and <u>go</u> [Gr] to the University of Pennsylvania. Last night we <u>go</u> [T] to the movies, but the movie wasn't very <u>exiting</u> [Sp].

<u>Do</u> [WW] you like to visit me? Why don't you come for a weekend?

I'd love to see you.

Write to me soon.

Love, Valeria

P.S. Here's my new e-mail address: Valet@intermail.net

3. Answer the questions.
   1. Where is Valeria? Where is she staying?
   2. Why is she there?
   3. What does she do each day?
   4. What does she do in her free time?
   5. Who has she met?

4. Imagine that you are a student in another town. Answer the questions in Exercise 3 about *you*.

5. Write a similar letter to a friend. Swap letters with a partner. Try to correct your partner's letter using the symbols.

UNIT 2 LETTERS AND E-MAILS – Formal and informal

1 Read lines 1–10 from some letters and e-mails. Which are formal and which are informal? Which are beginnings? Which are endings?

1. *Great to hear from you again.*
2. *I am writing in response to your advertisement in today's newspaper for an IT consultant.*
3. *Give my regards to Robert and all the family.*
4. *I'm sorry I haven't been in touch for so long, but you know how it is.*
5. *Thank you for your invoice of April 16th. Please find enclosed a check for the full amount.*
6. *Write, or better still, e-mail me soon.*
7. *We trust this arrangement meets with your satisfaction.*
8. *Just a note to say thank you so much for having me to stay last weekend.*
9. *Take care. I can't wait to see you next week.*
10. *I look forward to hearing from you at your earliest convenience.*

2 Read the **beginnings** of these letters and e-mails. Match them with their **next lines** and **endings**.

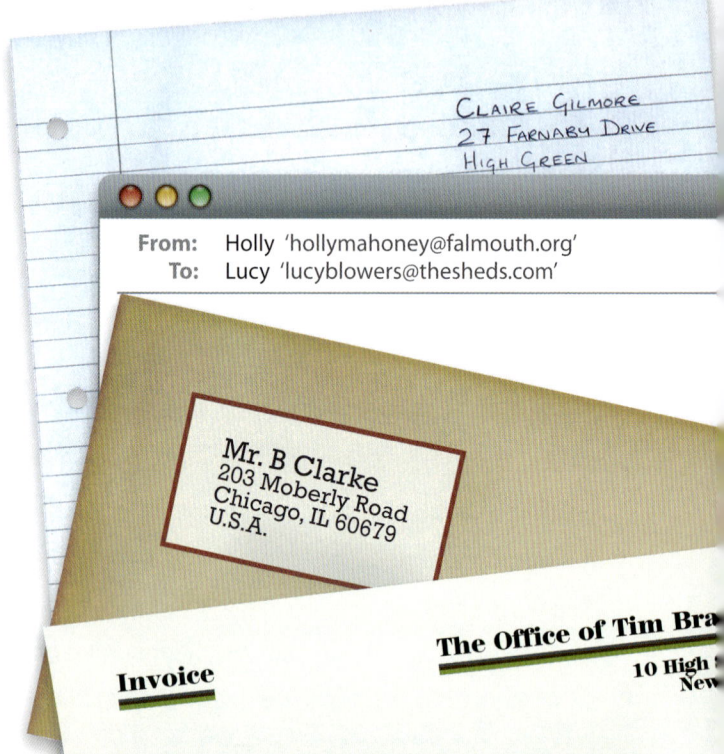

Beginnings	Next lines	Endings
1. Dear Jane, thanks for your e-mail. It's great to hear from you after so long.	a. We had no idea John was such a good cook!	e. Let me know a.s.a.p. All the best, Danny
2. Dear Mr. Smith, We have received your order and payment for the Children's Encyclopedia CD-ROM.	b. It's good to catch up on all your news. I've been pretty busy lately, too. I've just started a new job.	f. We apologize for the inconvenience. Your order will be processed as soon as we receive the additional amount. Yours sincerely, Pigeon Publishing
3. Hi Pete, Any chance you're free next Saturday evening?	c. Unfortunately, your check for $90 did not include postage of $7.50.	g. Let's meet soon. Give my love to Alan and the boys. Yours, Julie
4. Dear John and Liz, Thank you so much for a great evening and meal.	d. Chris and Nick are coming over and we wondered if you'd like to join us.	h. Thanks again. We hope to see you both soon. Love, Vicky and Jamie

3 Which letter or e-mail in Exercise 2 is …?
- an invitation
- a formal request
- exchanging news
- saying thank you

Underline the words or phrases which helped you decide.

4 You have just found the e-mail address of an old friend. Write to him/her. Give news about your personal life and work. Ask about his/her news.

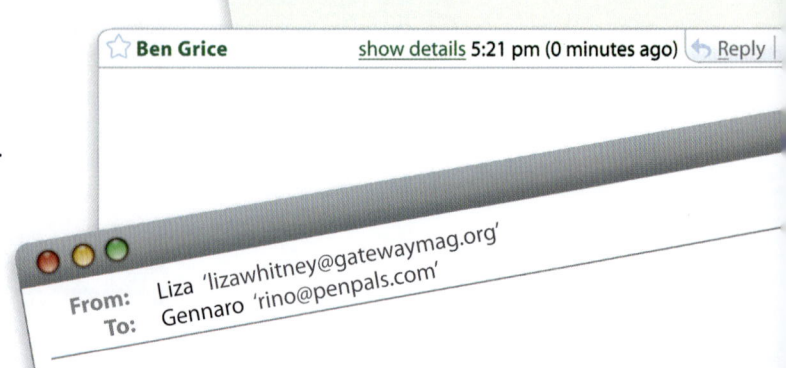

100 Writing Unit 2

UNIT 3 TELLING A STORY (1) – Linking ideas (1)

1 Read the story. Look at the picture. Who are the people?

The Farmer and his Sons

There was once an old, dying farmer **(1)** _____. Before he died, he wanted to teach his three sons how to be good farmers. So, he called them to his bedside and said, "My boys, I have an important secret to tell you: there is a great treasure buried in the vineyard. Promise me that you will look for it when I am dead."

The sons gave their promise and **(2)** _____, they began looking for the treasure. They worked very hard in the hot sun **(3)** _____. They pictured boxes of gold coins, diamond necklaces, and other such things. **(4)** _____, but they found not a single penny. They were very upset **(5)** _____. However, a few months later the grapes started to appear on the vines. Their grapes were the biggest and best in the neighborhood and they sold them for a lot of money. Now the sons understood **(6)** _____ and they lived happily ever after.

2 Where do clauses a–f go in the story?
- a. ☐ as soon as their father died
- b. ☐ who had worked hard in his vineyard all his life
- c. ☐ what their father had meant by the great treasure
- d. ☐ and while they were working, they thought about what their father had said
- e. ☐ because they felt that all their hard work had been for nothing
- f. ☐ Soon they had dug up every inch of the vineyard

3 Read the lines from another story. Who are the people in the picture?

The Emperor and his Daughters

There was once an emperor **(1)**_____ lived in a palace.
He had three daughters **(2)**_____ no sons.
He wanted his daughters to marry **(3)**_____ he died.
He found three princes. **(4)**_____ his daughters didn't like them.
They refused to marry the princes, **(5)**_____ the emperor became very angry.
He said they must get married **(6)**_____ they were 18 years old.
The three daughters ran away **(7)**_____ the night and found work on a farm.
They fell in love with the farmer's sons **(8)**_____ they were working there.
They married the sons **(9)**_____ they were 18.

4 Complete the lines using a linking word from the box.

before	as soon as	while	during
when	but	However,	so	who

5 In what ways are the lines below different from the ones in Exercise 3?

There was once an old emperor who lived in an enormous, golden palace in the middle of the city Ping Chong. He had three beautiful daughters, but unfortunately no sons ...

Continue rewriting the story, adding more detail to make it more interesting.

6 Write a folk tale or fairy story that you know. Write about 200 words.

Begin: *There was/were once ...*

End: *... and they lived happily ever after.*

Writing Unit 3 101

UNIT 4 A BIOGRAPHY – Combining sentences

Mother Teresa of Calcutta (1910–1997)

1 What do you know about Mother Teresa? Share ideas as a class.

2 Work with a partner. Look at the information about Mother Teresa's *Early years*. Compare the sentences in **A** with the paragraph in **B**. Note the different ways the sentences combine.

A Early years	B
Mother Teresa was a missionary. She worked among the poor people of Calcutta, India. She was born Agnes Gonxha Bojaxhiu. She was born in Skopje, Macedonia. She was born on August 26, 1910. Her father was Albanian. He died when she was eight years old. Her mother was left to raise the family.	Mother Teresa was a missionary who worked among the poor people of Calcutta, India. She was born Agnes Gonxha Bojaxhiu, in Skopje, Macedonia on August 26, 1910. Her father, who was Albanian, died when she was just eight years old, leaving her mother to raise the family.

3 Read the sentences in *Working as a teacher*. Work with your partner and use the information in **A** to complete the paragraph in **B**.

A Working as a teacher	B
Agnes was very young. She wanted to become a missionary. She left home in September 1928. She joined a convent in Ireland. She was given the name Teresa. She was sent to India in January 1929. She taught in St. Mary's High School Convent. St. Mary's was in Calcutta. She worked in St. Mary's for over 20 years. At first she was called Sister Teresa. She was called Mother Teresa in 1937.	From a very young age Agnes had wanted …, so in September 1928 she … to join … in Ireland, where she was given … . A few months later, in …, she was sent to … to teach in … in Calcutta. Here she worked for …, first as Sister … and finally, in 1937, as Mother Teresa.

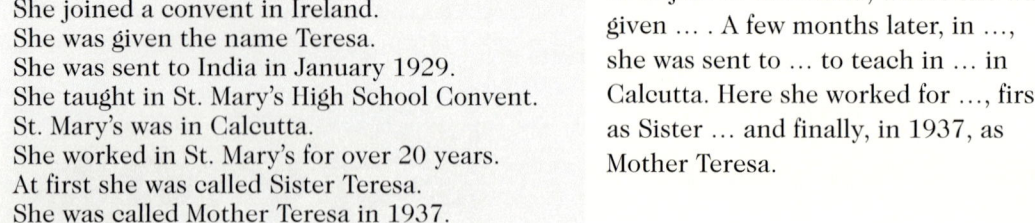

4 Do the same with the information in *Working with the poor*. Read your completed paragraph aloud to the class.

A Working with the poor	B
In 1946 Mother Teresa felt called by God. She was called to help the poorest of the poor. She left St. Mary's convent on August 17, 1948. She started visiting families in the slums of Calcutta. She looked after sick and dying children. She started a religious community in 1950. It was called the Missionaries of Charity. The communities spread all over the world in the 1960s and 70s. Mother Teresa was awarded the Nobel Peace Prize in 1979. She developed severe health problems. She continued to work amongst the poor. She died on September 5, 1997. Thousands of people from all over the world came to her funeral.	Mother Teresa finally left … on August 17, 1948. Two years earlier, in …, she had felt called by … to help…, so she started visiting …, looking … sick … . In 1950, she started … called the Missionaries of Charity, which by the 1960s and 70s had spread … . In 1979 Mother Teresa … . She continued to work … despite developing … . When she finally … on September 5, 1997, thousands of people … .

5 Research some facts about a famous man or woman, dead or alive, that you admire. Write a short biography.

UNIT 5 WRITING FOR TALKING

1 What topics are in the news at the moment? Are they national or international? Are they about the environment, politics, crime, sports …? Discuss any that concern you with the class.

2 **CD2 10** Read and listen to a girl talking about a topic that concerns her.
   1. What is her cause for concern?
   2. Why does she have a personal interest?
   3. How did Craig use to be?
   4. What does research tell us about the addiction?
   5. Do most children become addicts?
   6. What concerns Dr. Griffiths?
   7. What other concerns does the girl have?

3 Now read the speech carefully and answer the questions.
   1. Underline the phrases that introduce each paragraph. Why are these words used?
   2. Find examples of the speaker talking from her own experience.
   3. Find examples where she quotes research.
   4. How does the girl conclude her talk?
   5. Read the paragraph beginning "Research shows …" aloud to a partner.

Preparing your talk

4 Choose a cause for concern from the topics you discussed. Make notes. Say why it concerns you.

5 Write a speech to give to your class, of 200–300 words. Use your notes and these guidelines to help.
   1. Introduce your topic
      My cause for concern is …
      I want to talk about X because …
   2. Give the reason why
      Let me explain why.
      Two years ago …
      I've always been interested in …
   3. List your research
      Research shows that…
      A recent study found that …
      I read in the newspaper/heard on the news that …
   4. Introduce new points
      I have two more concerns.
      Firstly, … secondly, …
      Another thing is …
   5. Conclude
      Finally, I'd like to say …
      Thank you all very much for listening to me.
      Are there any questions?

My cause for concern

The thing I'm concerned about at the moment is the influence that video games may have on children.

Let me explain why. I've been reading lots of newspaper articles on the subject, and I also have a personal interest. You see, I have a younger brother, Craig; he's 13 years old, and I'm afraid he's becoming a video game addict. Just a few years ago, Craig had many interests. He played basketball, he was learning judo, he went out on his bike with his friends. He was a happy, fun-loving boy. Now he spends hours every day in front of a screen, in a virtual world, playing virtual games, usually violent ones, and he becomes really angry if our parents tell him to stop.

Research shows that today 40% of family homes have computers, so there is plenty of opportunity for very young children to start using them, and by the age of seven, many have developed an interest in video games. This is not a problem for most of them. However, by their early teens, a small minority have become addicts, playing for at least 30 hours a week. Dr. Mark Griffiths, an expert in video addiction, finds this figure very worrying. He says that children may become so addicted that they stop doing homework, start missing school, and even steal money in order to buy the games.

I have two more concerns. First, I worry that the violence in the games could cause children to become more violent. My brother isn't violent, but he is certainly bad-tempered if he is stopped from playing. Second, I worry that sitting without exercise for so long is unhealthy. Craig often plays five hours a day, and some days his thumbs are really sore and he can't sleep because he is overexcited. His schoolwork is going from bad to worse.

Finally, Dr. Griffiths says that more research is needed, but I don't need to read more research to conclude that video games cause problems. He should come and meet my brother. That's all the evidence he needs.

6 Practice reading your speech aloud first to yourself, then to a partner. Give your speech to the class. Answer any questions.

UNIT 6 DESCRIBING A PLACE – Relative pronouns and participles

1 Think of your favorite room. Draw a plan of it on a piece of paper. Write down why you like it and some adjectives to describe it.

My favorite room is . . .   I like it because . . .

Show a partner your plan and talk about your room.

2 Read the description "My favorite room." Why is this kitchen more than just a room where you cook and eat?

3 Complete the description using the relative clauses below:

... which tells the story
... that we're going to next Saturday
... where we cook and eat
... whose family has emigrated
... which is the focal point of the room
... which means
... we haven't seen
... I like best
... who are irritable and sleepy
... where family and friends come together

GRAMMAR SPOT

1 Underline the relative pronouns in Exercise 3. What do they refer to? When do we use *which*, *who*, *that*, *where*, and *whose*?

2 Look at the these sentences. We can omit the relative pronoun from one in each pair. Which one? Why?

This is the room **that** I like best.
This is the room **that** has the best view.

He's a friend **who** we haven't seen for years.
He's a friend **who** lives in London.

3 Look at these examples of participles. Rewrite them with relative pronouns.

I have so many happy memories of times spent there.
There is a large window looking out on two apple trees in the garden.

▶▶ Grammar Reference 6.3 and 6.4 p. 136

My favorite room

The room in our house (1) _____ is our kitchen. Perhaps the kitchen is the most important room in many houses, but it's particularly so in our house because it's not only (2) _____ but also the place (3) _____ .

I have so many happy memories of times spent there: ordinary daily events such as making breakfast on dark, cold winter mornings for children (4) _____ before sending them off to school; or special occasions such as family reunions or cooking holiday dinners. Whenever we have a party, people gravitate to the kitchen. It always ends up the fullest and noisiest room in the house.

So what does this special room look like? It's pretty big but not huge. It's big enough to have a good-sized rectangular table in the center, (5) _____ . There is a large window above the sink looking out on two apple trees in the garden. There's a big, old stove at one end and at the other end a wall with a huge bulletin board (6) _____ of our lives, past, present, and future: a school photo of the kids; a postcard from Aunt Nancy, (7) _____ to Canada; the menu from a takeout Chinese restaurant; an invitation to a wedding (8) _____ ; a letter from a friend (9) _____ for years. All our world is there for everyone to read!

The front door is seldom used in our house, only by strangers. All our friends use the back door, (10) _____ they come straight into the kitchen and join in whatever is happening there. Without doubt, some of the happiest times of my life have been spent in our kitchen.

4 Link these sentences with *who*, *which*, *that*, *where*, and *whose*.
  1. The blonde lady is Pat. She's wearing a black dress.
  2. There's the hospital. My sister works there.
  3. The postcard arrived this morning. It's from Aunt Nancy.
  4. I passed all my exams. This made my father very proud.
  5. Did you meet the girl? Her mother teaches Portuguese.

5 Complete the sentences with a word from the box in the present or past participle.

| play | give | stick |
| listen | arrange | |

  1. I spend hours in my room _____ to music.
  2. I have lots of posters _____ on the walls.
  3. My brother is in his bedroom _____ on his computer.
  4. There are photos of my family _____ on my shelves.
  5. I also have a color TV _____ to me on my last birthday.

6 Write about your favorite room. Use relative pronouns and participles.

Audio Scripts

UNIT 1

CD1 2 One World Quiz

1. In which country do men and women live the longest?
Women and men live longest in Japan. Women live on average 86 years and men 79. The average life expectancy in Japan is 81.25 years. In the U.S. it is 77.8 and in Germany 78.8.
2. In which year did the world population reach 6 billion?
The world population reached 6 billion in 1999. There are now over 6.5 billion people in the world.
3. If you are standing on the equator, how many hours of daylight do you have?
If you are standing at the equator you have 12 hours of daylight every day of the year. You also experience the fastest sunrise and sunset in the world, between 128 and 142 seconds depending on the time of year.
4. Where does most of the world's oil come from?
Most of the world's oil comes from Saudi Arabia. It produces 10.9 million barrels per day. Russia produces 9.4 million, and Venezuela 3.2 million.
5. Which of the seven wonders of the world is still standing?
Of the seven wonders of the ancient world only the pyramids of Egypt are still standing. The Colossus of Rhodes and the Lighthouse of Alexandria were destroyed by earthquakes hundreds of years ago.
6. Why didn't dinosaurs attack humans?
Dinosaurs didn't attack humans because they became extinct 65 million years ago. Human beings didn't appear on earth until 130,000 years ago.
7. Where was the Titanic sailing to when it sank?
The Titanic was sailing to New York from Southampton when it hit an iceberg on April 14th, 1912.
8. How long has Hawaii been a U.S. state?
Hawaii has been a U.S. state since 1959. It was the 50th state to be admitted to the union.
9. How many people have won the Nobel Peace prize since it started in 1901?
94 people have won the Nobel Peace prize since it started in 1901. These include Nelson Mandela in 1993 and Mother Teresa in 1979.
10. How long have people been using the Internet?
People have been using the Internet since 1969. It was invented by the U.S. Department of Defense as a means of communication. It first went live in October 1969, with communications between the University of California and the Stanford Research Institute.
11. Which language is spoken by the most people in the world?
Chinese is spoken by the most people in the world. Over one billion people speak it. English is the second most spoken language in the world, with about half a billion speakers.
12. In which country were women first given the vote?
New Zealand was the first country in the world to give women the vote in 1893. Canadian women were given the vote in 1917, but women in Paraguay weren't allowed to vote until 1961.

CD1 3 You're so wrong!

1. A The Pope lives in Montreal.
   B He doesn't live in Montreal! He lives in Rome. In the Vatican.
2. A Shakespeare didn't write poems.
   B You're wrong. He wrote hundreds of poems, not just plays.
3. A Vegetarians eat meat.
   B Of course they don't eat meat. They only eat vegetables and sometimes fish.
4. A The Internet doesn't provide much information.
   B That's not true! It provides a lot. Sometimes I think that it provides too much!
5. A The world is getting colder.
   B It isn't getting colder, it's getting hotter. Haven't you heard of global warming?
6. A John F. Kennedy was traveling by plane when he was killed.
   B No, you're wrong. He wasn't traveling by plane. He was traveling by car, in Dallas, Texas.
7. A Brazil has never won the World Cup.
   B Brazil *has* won it, five times. My dad goes on about it all the time.
8. A The 2008 Olympics were held in Tokyo.
   B No, they weren't held in Tokyo. They were held in China, in Beijing.

CD1 4 is or has?

1. My brother's just started a new job.
2. He's working in South America.
3. He's been there three months.
4. He's having a great time.
5. He's never worked overseas before.
6. His company's called Intext Worldwide.

CD1 5 Making conversation

R = Ruth (mother)   N = Nick (son)
L = Lily (daughter)
R So kids, did you have a good day at school?
N No.
L Yes, I did. We were practicing for the school concert.
R Oh, wonderful! Do you have a lot of homework?
L Ugh! Yes, I do. I have Geography, Spanish, and Math! Do you have a lot, Nick?
N Yeah.
R Nick, did you remember your soccer uniform?
N Um …
L No, he didn't. He forgot it again.
R Oh, Nick, you know we need to wash it. Are you playing soccer tomorrow?
N No.
R Lily, do you need your uniform tomorrow?
L Yes, I do. I have a softball game after school. We're playing our rival team.
R Didn't they beat you last time?
L Yes, they did. But we'll beat them tomorrow.
N No, you won't! Your team's terrible.
R OK. That's enough, children. Put on your seatbelts! Let's go!

CD1 6

R So kids, did you have a good day at school?
N No, I didn't. Not really. We didn't have any of my favorite subjects.
L Yes, I did. We were practicing for the school concert.
R Oh, wonderful! Do you have a lot of homework?
L Ugh! Yes, I do. I have Geography, Spanish, and Math! Do you have a lot, Nick?
N Yes, I do. I have to work on my science project. I have to finish by Friday!
R Nick, did you remember your soccer uniform?
N Oh no, I didn't—sorry, Mom.
R Oh, Nick, you know we need to wash it. Are you playing soccer tomorrow?
N No, I'm not, thank goodness. The game was cancelled.
R Lily, do you need your uniform tomorrow?
L Yes, I do. I have a softball game after school. We're playing our rival team.
R Didn't they beat you last time?
L Yes, they did. But we'll beat them tomorrow.
N Ummm—I'm not so sure about that.
R OK. That's enough, children. Put on your seatbelts! Let's go!

CD1 7 see page 5

CD1 8 A world in one family

An interview with Xavier
I So, Xavier—how old are you?
X I'm 21.
I And I know you have an interesting background. What nationality are you?
X Well, I have an American passport …
I … so you're American, but your parents—what nationality are your parents?
X Well, my dad's Peruvian. He was born in Peru, in South America, but he's had an American passport for the last 20 years. My mom was born in Spain, in the Basque country, and she still has her Spanish passport.
I So, how did they meet and end up having children in the U.S.?
X Ummm … they met when they were both studying English in the U.S. Ummm … and um … and about three years after that that they got married and here I am, and then my brother.
I And what was it like growing up in the U.S. with a Spanish mother and a Peruvian father?
X I don't think I actually noticed nationality for years—um … probably the first time I really noticed a difference was in high school. The U.S. was playing Spain in the 2004 Olympic Games, and my classmates made me choose which country to support.
I So which country did you support?
X I stayed neutral. Actually, I didn't care which team won.
I And which nationality do you feel now?
X I'd say I was American—um, but I'm also very proud of my parents' heritage, half Basque and half Peruvian. I like that.
I What contact have you had with your family abroad?
X Well, I've only actually been to Spain once—um, when I was a baby. I've had more contact on my dad's side. My Peruvian grandparents visit us in the U.S., and when I was growing up, we always went to Peru in the summer, and …
I Very nice.
X … and if I'm home I speak to them—um, to my grandparents, on the phone—um … maybe once a week.
I And do you think that your Spanish heritage has influenced you at all?
X Well, yes, I think so. I think it influenced my degree choice. I'm studying modern languages at Syracuse University—Spanish and French. I'm in my third year. I have one more year to do.

I And what are you hoping to do in the future?
X Umm—That's a very good question. Um … hopefully a job that offers some kind of opportunity to travel, but ultimately, I want to settle down for good in the U.S. I've always been interested in my background, but I think that I realize the U.S. is my home and it is where I see myself living.
I Thank you very much, Xavier.
X You're welcome.

CD1 9 I = Interviewer   A = Ana
I Ana, you're Spanish, aren't you?
A Yes, I am. I'm from Bilbao, in the Basque country.
I And how long have you lived here in New York?
A Um … 23 years.
I And how did that happen?
A Well, I wanted to improve my English so I came to the U.S. to study. Originally, I came for six months but—um … I met my husband—um … we met at college—actually we met on the way to the college, in the street.
I You met in the street?
A Yes, it was the first day and I was walking up the hill to the college, and Teo, that's my husband, was driving up the hill, and he stopped and offered me a ride, which I refused.
I You refused?
A Yes, but we ended up in the same class. I went into the class, and there he was.
I And your husband's from Peru, isn't he?
A Yes, he is.
I So that means you speak the same language.
A Yes, Spanish.
I So, why did you decide to live in the U.S.?
A Well, mainly because my husband had a job here and, um—we kind of decided we wanted a place in the middle, between Spain and Peru.
I A nice idea. And you have two sons.
A Yes, I do. Xavier is 21, nearly 22, and James is 19.
I So, what's it been like for them growing up in the U.S. with parents of different nationality?
A Well, I think because we live in New York, a cosmopolitan city, they didn't notice it too much.
I They are both bilingual presumably?
A No, not really.
I Oh.
A … because, when they were children, even though we spoke to them in Spanish, they always replied in English.
I Um, interesting. Tell me, how much contact has your family here had with the families in Spain and Peru?
A I think more with my husband's family in Peru because it's closer. We always spent summer there—um—two or three weeks usually.
I And the Spanish side?
A Well, I keep in touch all the time, but my family has never been here.
I Never?
A Never. We went to Spain once when Xavier was 18 months old. James has never been.
I So what are the children doing now?
A Xavier's in college and James just finished high school. He's been working in a restaurant, saving money to travel.
I And what do they want to do in the future?
A Well, James, he's going to travel to Spain at last! Then he's going to college to study Biology.
I And Xavier?
A I think he wants to work in foreign affairs.
I Ana, is it possible to sum up the pros and cons of bringing up a family in another country?
A Well, I think in a way it's good because you can take the best things from both cultures, but I don't think my sons will ever feel 100% American because their parents aren't American. It's very tricky.

CD1 10 Pronunciation
1. rose   goes   does   toes
2. meat   beat   great   street
3. paid   made   played   said
4. done   phone   son   won

CD1 11
mother   enjoy   apartment   holiday   population

CD1 12 Everyday situations
1. **A** I need to make an appointment. It's pretty urgent. I've lost a filling.
   B We have a cancellation this afternoon. 2:45, if that's OK?
   A That's great. I'll be there.
2. **A** A medium latte and a muffin, please.
   B For here or to go?
   A Here, please.
   B That'll be $3.90 please.
3. **A** I can't make the meeting. I'm stuck in traffic.
   B Don't worry. We'll start without you and brief you later.
   A Oh, hold on! We're moving again. I should be there in about an hour.
4. **A** Can you put in your PIN number and press "Enter"?
   B Oh, no! I can't remember my number for this card. Oh, what is it?
   A Do you have another card you could use?
5. **A** Bottled or tap? And do you want ice and lemon in it?
   B Bottled, please. Ice but no lemon.
   A No problem. Is that all?
6. **A** I don't think you've met Greg. He's joining us from our New York office.
   B Hello. Good to meet you. I've heard a lot about you.
   C Yeah, at last we meet. I'm looking forward to working together.
7. **A** How many bags are you checking in?
   B Just the one.
   A And did you pack it yourself?
   B Yes, I did.
8. **A** The elevator's on your right. Would you like someone to help you with your bags?
   B No, thank you. I'll manage.
   A OK. If you insist. Here's your key. Enjoy your stay.
9. **A** Please hold. Your call is important to us. All our operators are busy at the moment, but one of them will be with you shortly.
   B If I have to listen to that again, I'll go crazy!
   C Can I help you?
   B At last a real person! Do you know how long I've been waiting?
10. **A** There are still tickets for the 5:45 performance, but the 8:45 is sold out, I'm afraid.
    B That's fine. We'll have two, please, one adult, one child.
    A OK. Two for 5:45. The doors open at 5.

CD1 13 Role play
1. **A** Maria, this is my friend Peter. We came to the U.S. together. We come from the same town in Canada.
   B Hello, Peter. Nice to meet you. I hope you're having a good time.
2. **A** Excuse me. I don't think this is mine. I ordered a medium latte and a muffin.
   B Oh, sorry. My mistake. This is for the next table.
3. **A** Good evening. Reception? I'm in room 216, and my TV isn't working. Can you send someone to fix it?
   B Of course, sir. I'll send someone immediately.
4. **A** Excuse me. Can you tell me which is the check-in desk for Bangkok? I can't see my flight on the screen.
   B Oh no. You're at the wrong terminal. Flights to Bangkok leave from Terminal 2. You can take a bus to the terminal over there.
5. **A** OK, everyone. Dinner's ready! Can you all come to the table? Bring your drinks and just help yourselves to the food.
   BCD Mmmm. It smells good. Can we sit where we like?

UNIT 2

CD1 14 "Blue Monday" by Fats Domino
Blue Monday, how I hate Blue Monday
Got to work like a slave all day
Here come Tuesday, oh hard Tuesday
I'm so tired got no time to play

On Wednesday, work twelve hours, then
Go home, fall into bed at ten
'Cause Thursday is a hard working day
And Friday I get my pay

Saturday morning, oh, Saturday morning
All my tiredness has gone away
Got my money and my honey
And I'm out on the town to play

Sunday morning my head is bad,
But it's worth it for the fun that I had
Sunday evening it's goodnight and amen
'Cause on Monday I start again

CD1 15 My favorite day of the week
Vicky
I go to a boarding school, so I don't live with my parents during the semester. Um … what I like is being with my friends all the time. Whether we're working or just chatting, it's great to know there's always someone there. There's also a lot of freedom. I don't have to tell my parents where I'm going, who I'm going with, you know … Normally Monday is my favorite day because I only have two classes on Mondays, but I'm having a very bad day today because I have homework from every one of my teachers, and I have to do it now!

Terry
I work in a restaurant in Miami. I have two days off a week, usually Monday and Wednesday, but my favorite day of the week is in fact Friday, even though I work that day. It's the best night because all my friends come into the restaurant, and we have a great time. There's a real buzz to the place, and it doesn't feel like work at all. Time just flies by. The restaurant's being redecorated right now, so everything's a little crazy.

Dave
I'm a police officer. I like my job because it's challenging, but I live for surfing. I go as often as I can. I'm opening two shops that sell surfboards in the next few months. The boards are made here in the U.S. Sunday is my favorite day of the week. I hardly ever work on Sundays. I get up as early as I can, and spend the day at the beach.

Jenny
Mike and I live on a beautiful farm in Missouri. I know we're very lucky, but it's hard work. We never have a day off on weekends or holidays, or any day of the year. We have to feed the animals and take care of the fields. Now we're harvesting, so we aren't getting any rest at all. But I suppose our favorite day is Wednesday because that's the day we generally get together with friends and prepare a wonderful meal.

CD1 16 Dave Telford, police officer and surfer

What's your background?

D I'm 35, and I'm single. I live in Los Angeles, California. I'm a police officer. I've been in the police force for over ten years. I love my job, but my passion is surfing.

What hours do you work?

D I work different shifts. The morning shift starts at 5:00, and I can't stand that because I have to get up at 4:30. My favorite shift is 2:00 in the afternoon until midnight because I get home about 12:30. What's good is that I work ten hours a day for four days then have three days off.

What do you think of your job?

D My job is extremely busy and very hard. But I like it because it's challenging, and I never know what's going to happen. I like working in a team. We look after each other and work together.

Why do you like surfing?

D My work is very stressful, so I surf to get away from it all. It's just me and the sea, and my mind switches off. I concentrate so hard on what I'm doing that I don't think about anything else.

How often do you go surfing?

D I go surfing whenever I'm not working. Sometimes I'm on the beach before 7:00 in the morning. I go all over the world surfing. Next month I'm going to Costa Rica, and in the fall I'm going to Thailand.

Do you have a business?

D I have a surfing school. I teach all ages, from kids to seniors. The business is doing well. I'm also opening two shops that sell surfboards. The boards are made here in the U.S.

What is your favorite day of the week?

D I like Sundays best of all. I work as a lifeguard, then around 6:00 me and my friends barbecue some burgers and relax. Awesome! I've been all around the world, but when I look around me, I think there's nowhere else I'd rather be.

CD1 17 Questions and answers

1. Where does he live?
   In Los Angeles, California.
2. Is he married?
   No, he is single.
3. Why doesn't he like the morning shift?
   Because he has to get up at 4:30.
4. How many hours a day does he work?
   Ten.
5. What does he like about his job?
   He likes it because it's challenging, and he likes working in a team.
6. What does he think about while he's surfing?
   He only thinks about surfing, nothing else.
7. Where's he going next month?
   Costa Rica.
8. Is his business doing well?
   Yes, it is. He's opening two shops.
9. What do he and his friends do on Sunday evenings?
   They eat burgers and relax.

CD1 18 The office

A = new employee B = established employee

A Gosh! I don't know anybody! Can you help me? Who are all these people?
B Uh, well, that's Simon. He's sitting at the head of the table reading something.
A He's the one wearing a sweater, right?
B Yeah, that's him.
A And what does he do?
B He's the Managing Director. He's the man in charge.
A The boss, in other words.
B Uh-huh. He shouts a lot, but he listens as well. Then there's Edward. He's wearing a suit. He's standing up talking to Anna. Edward's the sales director. He's charming. He always has a nice word to say to everyone. Anna's standing next to him. She's drinking coffee. She's wearing a jacket and she has a scarf around her neck.
A And Anna is the …?
B Anna's the accountant. Money, money, money. Very bright, very quick.
A Oh, OK. And who's that talking on her phone?
B In the blue skirt? That's Jenny, the Human Resources Manager, HR manager. She deals with all the personnel. She's a sweetheart. Everyone loves her. Then there's Matthew. He's the IT manager. He's only working here for a few months. He's from our New York office. I don't really know him very well.
A He's the guy working on his laptop?
B That's him. Wearing a shirt, no tie. He knows everything about technology. And finally that's Christina talking to Simon. She's his PA. She …
A Sorry. What was that?
B She's Simon's PA, Personal Assistant. She organizes his schedule, but she helps all of us, really. We couldn't cope without her. She runs the whole place, actually. She's the one in a black suit and fabulous earrings. Very sharp.
A Right. I think I got that …

CD1 19 Who earns how much?

Part 1

A Well, I guess that doctors earn a lot.
B Yeah. I think so, too. They have a lot of responsibility and a lot of training. I'd say that doctors get about … $140,000? What do you think?
A Could be … or it could be even more, $200,000.
B One of those two, anyway. Should we look at the high earners first?
A Uh-huh. $750,000 …
B There's one higher …
A Oh, is there? Oh, yes. A million. Mmm.
B I'd say … that has to be the basketball player.
A Yes, definitely. They do earn ridiculous amounts of money, don't they? So what about $750,000? Who earns three quarters of a million?
B Um … I think that's the lawyer.
A As much as that? What about the Senior Director? Do lawyers earn more than them?
B Maybe, maybe not. I suppose the lawyer could be $140,000, and the Senior Director $750,000. Senior Directors are in charge of huge companies.
A OK. Now … the pilot. Pilots earn a lot, don't they? They need a lot of experience. They have people's lives in their hands … I think they get … oh, at least a hundred, a hundred fifty.
B Mmm. I know what you mean, but I don't think they get that much.
A Don't they? Oh! Anyway, there isn't 150 on this list, so …
B I guess pilots get about $65,000 …
A OK. I'd say that's about right …

CD1 20

Part 2

B Let's go on down to the bottom. What's the lowest salary?
A $20,000. I guess that's the nurse. They don't get paid much, nurses.
B I thought they earned more than that, actually. I know they don't get much, but even so …
A Then there's $25,000, and the next up is $30,000.
B Oh, look! Supermarket cashier. I don't suppose they get much. $25,000, I'd say?
A OK. That seems about right. What about farmers? How much do they get?
B I don't know. It depends what sort of farmer. They can earn a fortune, can't they?
A I suppose so, yes … But they're always complaining that supermarkets don't pay them enough for what they produce.
B I still think they get a decent salary. They own so much land! I bet they get 50 or 60 thousand.
A No, I think it's much lower. I'd say $30,000.
B Hmm. Not so sure. Then we have … teachers. What do they earn?
A I guess they get … um … $40,000?
B But it all depends how many years they've worked and how many qualifications they have.
A Yes, I know, but we're talking about the average.
B Don't teachers and police officers earn about the same?
A Do they? I'm not so sure. I'd say that police officers get more. What do we have? $40,000 … $48,000.
B I think 40 for the police officer and 48 for the teacher.
A Well, actually I'd say the other way around. 48 for the police officer and 40 for the teacher. My mother's a teacher, and she doesn't earn anything like that!
B What does that leave? We haven't decided about the farmer or the nurse yet.
A I think the nurse gets less than the farmer. She gets the least.
B Why she? Nurses can be men, you know.
A True. Sorry. Nurses—men *and* women—earn less than farmers.
B Men AND women.
A Absolutely.

CD1 21 Free time activities

John
My favorite hobby is cooking, and that's a thing you do at home, obviously. I cook most days, though not every day. We also like eating out. What clothes and equipment do I need? Well, I always wear an apron to protect my clothes, because you can make a mess when you're cooking, and tomatoes and spices change the color of your clothes forever! The most important piece of equipment is knives, and I'm very particular about my knives. They're German, and very sharp, and I really take care of them. Obviously in the kitchen you need all sorts of things like pots and pans and baking dishes and chopping boards and food mixers, but I don't really have a lot of gadgets. I like to keep things simple. What I like about cooking is the fact that it's creative and it's real. We have to eat, and what we eat is really important, so I like to know that what I'm eating, and what my family is eating, is good. I actually like all the preparation. Going out shopping, seeing the food, feeling it, smelling it, talking to the people who are selling it, is half the fun. People often ask me what I like cooking, and I don't really have an answer. Whatever looks good, and whatever I feel like cooking that day. The best part is of course seeing people enjoy my food, but what's also very important to me is seeing everyone happy, and enjoying being at the table. It's about the occasion as much as the food.

CD1 22

A = Ann J = Joaquim

A So what do you think of Chicago, Joaquim?
J It's really interesting. Chicago's such a great city. There are some beautiful buildings, and the people are so friendly!
A Yes, they are. When did you get here?
J Two days ago. I took a flight from Miami. We were a bit late landing, but it didn't matter.
A Oh, good. Where are you staying in Chicago?
J At the Avenue Hotel. It's very convenient for the office. My room isn't very big, but it's OK.
A That's too bad! Don't worry. Where are you from?
J From Brazil. I was born in São Paulo, but I live in a suburb of Rio de Janeiro. It's very pretty, and it's not far from the sea.

Audio Scripts 116

A Really? It sounds beautiful. Your English is very good. Where did you learn it?
J That's very kind of you, but I know I make a lot of mistakes. I learned it in school for years, and I've been to the U.S. many times.
A Oh, have you? How interesting! And what are you doing here in Chicago, Joaquim?
J I'm attending a conference. I'm here for five days, and I'm going home on the 17th.
A Oh, so soon! And have you managed to get around our city yet?
J I haven't seen very much. I've been for a walk along the lakefront path and I've taken a boat tour from the Navy Pier, but I haven't been to the John Hancock Observatory yet.
A Well, I hope you enjoy it. Don't work too hard!
J I'll try to enjoy myself! Bye. It was nice to talk to you.

CD1 23
1. Who do you work for?
2. Do you enjoy your job?
3. Where do you come from?
4. Have you been to New York?
5. What do you do when you're not working?
6. The weather's amazing right now, isn't it?
7. Are you going on vacation this year?
8. This city's very exciting, isn't it?
9. What's your favorite TV show?

CD1 24
1. A Who do you work for?
   B Siemens. I've been with them for four years. They're a good company. How about you?
2. A Do you enjoy your job?
   B Yes, I do. It's quite hard, but it's very challenging. I don't earn very much. What about you? Do you like your job?
3. A Where do you come from?
   B I was born in Michigan, and I've lived there all my life with my parents. I'd like to live abroad some time.
4. A Have you been to New York?
   B No, I haven't, but I'd love to. I've heard it's one of the most amazing cities in the world. Have you been there?
5. A What do you do when you're not working?
   B Well, I like horseback riding, and I play golf. And I love music, so I often go to concerts. Do you?
6. A The weather's amazing right now, isn't it?
   B Yes, it's so mild. We haven't had any real cold weather at all! Have you heard a weather forecast for the weekend? It's supposed to be good, isn't it?
7. A Are you going on vacation this year?
   B Yes, I'm going to Mexico with some friends. I haven't been there before, so I'm really looking forward to it. What about you?
8. A This city's very exciting, isn't it?
   B Really? Do you think so? There isn't very much to do. I get so bored here. What *do* you find to do?
9. A What's your favorite TV show?
   B I like soaps and documentaries. And game shows. And the news. I suppose I like everything. What about you?

UNIT 3

CD1 25 Vincent Van Gogh
1. Where was he born?
2. What was his job?
3. Why was he fired?
4. Why did he try to commit suicide?
5. Which artists did he meet?
6. What was he doing when he met them?
7. Who came to live with him?
8. Where did they first meet?
9. What was he carrying?
10. Why did he cut off part of his ear?
11. Which paintings were completed there?
12. What was he doing when he shot himself?
13. Why did he shoot himself?
14. Where was he buried?
15. Why didn't he have any money?

CD1 26
1. Where was he born?
   In Brabant in the Netherlands.
2. What was his job?
   He worked as an art dealer.
3. Why was he fired?
   Because he'd had an argument with customers.
4. Why did he try to commit suicide?
   Because he'd fallen in love with his cousin and she'd rejected him.
5. Which artists did he meet?
   Degas, Pissarro, Seurat, Toulouse-Lautrec, Monet, and Renoir.
6. What was he doing when he met them?
   He was studying art.
7. Who came to live with him?
   Gauguin.
8. Where did they first meet?
   In Paris.
9. What was he carrying?
   A razor blade.
10. Why did he cut off part of his ear?
    Because he'd had an argument with Gauguin.
11. Which paintings were completed there?
    Starry Night, Irises, and *Self-Portrait Without a Beard.*
12. What was he doing when he shot himself?
    He was painting outside.
13. Why did he shoot himself?
    Because he was depressed.
14. Where was he buried?
    In Auvers.
15. Why didn't he have any money?
    Because he'd sold only one of his paintings.

CD1 27 see page 19

CD1 28
/t/ worked published
/d/ tried moved continued died recognized
/ɪd/ rejected completed

CD1 29 I didn't do much
1. I didn't do much. I just had something to eat, watched TV for a while, and then had an early night. I was in bed by ten.
2. I went to my yoga class, then went out to eat with a couple of friends. I got home about nine and did a bit of housework, and that was it.
3. I went out with some people from work, so I didn't get home until about midnight. Well, after midnight, actually. It was a very late night for me!
4. I met some friends in town for coffee, and we talked for a while. Then I went home and did some stuff on the computer, you know, Facebook, then went to bed about eleven thirty.

CD1 30 Smash! Clumsy visitor destroys priceless vases

A clumsy visitor to a museum has destroyed a set of priceless 300-year-old Chinese vases after slipping on the stairs.
The three vases, which were produced during the Qing dynasty in the 17th century, had stood on a windowsill at the City Museum for forty years. Last Thursday they were smashed into a million pieces. The vases, which were donated in 1948, had been the museum's best known pieces.
The museum decided not to identify the man who had caused the disaster. "It was a most unfortunate and regrettable accident," museum director Duncan Robinson said, "but we are glad that the visitor wasn't seriously injured."
The photograph was taken by another visitor, Steve Baxter. "We watched the man fall as if in slow motion. He was flying through the air. The vases exploded as though they had been hit by a bomb. The man was sitting there stunned in the middle of a pile of porcelain when the staff arrived."
The museum declined to say what the vases were worth.

CD1 31 I = Interviewer   NF = Nick Flynn
I It's 7:45, and you're listening to the *Morning Show*. The man who broke Chinese vases worth $160,000 when he fell down the stairs at a museum has been identified by a daily newspaper. He's Nick Flynn, and he's with us now. Are you all right, Mr. Flynn? You didn't hurt yourself falling down the stairs, did you?
NF I'm recovering, which is more than I can say for the vases!
I Very true! How did it happen?
NF I was coming down the stairs, looking at the pictures, and I slipped. The stairs are very slick, and it had been raining, so I guess my shoes were a bit wet. And I just went head over heels.
I It must have been a strange feeling, lying in the middle of all that priceless porcelain?
NF I was surprised that these incredibly valuable vases were left just lying on a windowsill. I'd seen them lots of times before, but I hadn't really paid them any attention.
I And I hear you've been banned from the museum? Is that right?
NF Yes, I got a letter from the director of the museum asking me not to go back. It's a shame, because I used to go twice a week. Now I have to find somewhere else to go.
I Well, thank you, Mr. Flynn, and good luck.

CD1 32 see page 21

CD1 33 Words that sound the same
knew/new   read/red   wore/war   threw/through
flew/flu

CD1 34 see page 21

CD1 35 see page 21

CD1 36 see page 21

CD1 37 see page 22

CD1 38 The first time I fell in love
Sarah
The first time I fell in love was when I was 13. It was with a boy named Max. We were on a school trip, a geography trip, so a whole group of us were traveling together for a week. I'd never really noticed this boy before, because we used to hang out with different people, but I suddenly started looking at him, and I remember thinking, "Hmm! You're nice!" and I couldn't understand why I hadn't looked at him before. He was very quiet, and he had dark eyes that seemed to see everything, and he made me go all weak at the knees. We kind of started going out. When we held hands, it was electric! I'd never felt anything like it in my life! Wow! I don't think he felt the same way. He was very cool about everything. It only lasted a few months. Then he went back to his friends and I went back to mine.

Tommy

T Well, I fell in love with a girl called Clara, but it didn't last very long.
I How long did it last?
T Well … about two weeks. It all ended last Friday.
I Really? What happened last Friday?
T I decided that I'd had enough of being in love. I didn't like the feeling.
I Was Clara upset?
T Not really. She didn't know anything about it.
I What?
T No. I hadn't told her that I was in love with her, so she didn't know that it had ended.
I Was it so bad?
T Oh, yes. I couldn't sleep, I used to get this funny feeling here in my tummy when I saw her coming, and my heart went bang, bang, bang. It was horrible!
I So how did you manage to stop loving her?
T Well, I'm only 9, and I figured that I'm too young to only love one person for the rest of my life.
I Fair enough. I'm glad you didn't hurt her feelings.
T I'm glad it's all over.

James

Well, I've only been in love once in my life, and that was when I was 22. I'd had other girlfriends, of course, but it was never more than that. Just a girlfriend. And then I met this other girl, Ruth, and my whole life just turned upside down. I remember thinking at the time that I'd never felt anything like it. Nothing looked the same, felt the same, life had never been so amazing, so colorful. I wanted to do everything—climb mountains, fly like a bird, stay up all night—life was far too amazing to sleep. It's funny, I never used to care what I looked like, but suddenly I started to care. I wanted to look good for this girl in my life. I felt that I hadn't really lived until that moment, until I'd met her and fallen in love. Thank goodness she felt the same! We're still together. Fifteen years and four kids later. Amazing, huh?

CD1 39 see page 25

CD1 40

1. We had a great time in Thailand, didn't we?
2. The weather was great, wasn't it?
3. The French really love their food, don't they?
4. It's a lovely day today, isn't it?
5. Karen and Tom are a really nice couple, aren't they?
6. Tom earns so much money, doesn't he?
7. They want to get married, don't they?

CD1 41

1. A She's very nice.
   B She's absolutely wonderful!
2. A The movie was good.
   B The movie was just great!
3. A The hotel's all right.
   B The hotel's really fabulous!
4. A I like dark chocolate.
   B I absolutely adore dark chocolate.
5. A I like Peter.
   B I really love Peter.
6. A The book wasn't very good.
   B The book was absolutely awful!
7. A I don't like noisy restaurants.
   B I just can't stand noisy restaurants!

UNIT 4

CD1 42 Discussing grammar

1. I don't get along with my boss. Do you think I should look for another job?
2. We're throwing Tom a surprise birthday party. You can't tell him about it.
3. Please, Dad, can I go to Tom's party? It'll be great.
4. You have to drive on the left in England.
5. Do you have to wear a uniform in your job?
6. Are you allowed to take cell phones to school?
7. I had to go to bed early when I was a child.
8. You don't have to go to the U.S. to learn English, but it's a good idea.

CD1 43 Giving advice

Conversation 1

A Are you going to Charlotte's party?
B I don't know if I should go or not.
A What do you mean?
B Well, her parents are abroad, and they told her she wasn't allowed to have friends over while they were away.
A Oh, come on! You have to come. It's a party. Everyone has parties when their parents are away.
B Yeah, but her mom and dad are best friends with mine.
A Look. You don't have to tell your mom and dad. Just go to the party and help clean up after.
B I'm not sure.

Conversation 2

A Do you see that woman over there?
B Yeah, what about her?
A She's eating!
B So?
A You're not allowed to eat in this store.
B Well …
A Do you think I should tell her to stop?
B No, no, you shouldn't say anything. It's embarrassing. The sales assistant will tell her.
A No! I can't just sit here. I have to say something. Um—excuse me …

Conversation 3

A I'm so mad!
B Why?
A I got a parking ticket. I had to go to the store for my dad, and when I got back to the car, there was ticket on the windshield.
B Oh, that's bad luck!
A I think *he* should pay the fine.
B Who? Your dad? Why? He wasn't driving.
A Yeah, but I was doing *his* shopping.
B But he didn't tell you to park illegally.
A OK, OK, so it's my fault. Um—I still think he should pay it.

CD1 44

Rules for life

1. Millie

Well, so many teenagers seem to think life is about just one thing, you know—money and fame, they think it will bring them happiness. Honestly, I would hate to be famous. When I read the magazines and see all the photos of these rich, famous movie stars, athletes and the like, it frightens me. They can't move without being followed and photographed. Usually they have bodyguards. When I grow up I just want to enjoy my work. If I earn lots of money, fair enough, but if I don't, I'll still be happy. I never want to be famous. That's scary stuff.

2. Richard

My rule for life is that you only get out of life what you put in. I mean, you should never ask that question people always ask "Why are we here? What is the meaning of life?"—you'll never find the answer. You've got to *give* meaning to your life by what you *do* with your life—um … and I think you can do this in all kinds of ways. It doesn't matter if you are president of your country or a janitor. You have a place in the world, you have a part to play.

3. Frank

I believe you've got to look for the good in people and things. So many people of my age do nothing but complain about today's world—oh, on and on they go about—ooh, how bad the traffic is, or how cell phones are such a menace. Oh, and most of all they complain about young people—they're loud, they're impolite, not like in the "good old days." Well, I don't agree with all that. There's always been good and bad in the world, and I think we should look for the good. The rule I try to live by is find three things every day to be happy about.

CD1 45 Spoken English

1. "Isn't your mom away this week?"
   "Yeah, so Dad's got to do all the cooking, and I've got to do the ironing."
2. "Where's my briefcase? I've got to go to work."
   "It's where you left it when you came home. In the hallway by the front door."
3. "Mom, why can't I go out now?"
   "You've got to clean up your room first. Your friends will just have to wait."
4. "Won't you be late for work?"
   "Oh, no. Look at the time. I've got to go now. We'll catch up later. Bye!"

CD1 46 "I Believe"

I believe in bottle banks
And beauty from within
I believe in saying thanks
And fresh air on the skin

I believe in healthy walks
As tonic for the feet
I believe in serious talks
And just enough to eat

Chorus
That's what I believe
Surprising as it seems
I believe that happiness
Is well within our dreams

I believe in being nice
In spite of what you think
I believe in good advice
And not too much to drink

I believe in being true
In everything you try to do
I believe in me and you
I hope you share my point of view

Chorus
I believe in being kind
Especially when it's hard
I believe an open mind
Can show a fine regard

I believe that manners make
A person good to know
I believe in birthday cake
And going with the flow

Chorus
That's what I believe
Although it seems naïve
I believe that peace and love
Are there to be achieved

That's what I believe …

CD1 47 Phrasal verbs

1. A Who do you take after in your family?
   B Mmm … I don't think I take after anyone in particular. Although the older I get, the more I think I'm like my mother. Humph!
2. A Do you get along with both your parents?
   B Yes, I do. Most of the time. I do a lot of stuff with my dad. Baseball and things.

3. A Have you recently taken up any new sports or hobbies?
   B Me? No! My life's too busy already!
4. A Do you often look up words in your dictionary?
   B Sometimes, if I'm really stuck.
5. A Are you looking forward to going on vacation soon?
   B I wish! But I just went on vacation, so I have to wait until the holidays now.
6. A Do you pick up foreign languages easily?
   B Well, I picked up Italian quite easily when I was living in Milan, but I already knew Spanish, so I think that helped a little.
7. A Do you have any bad habits that you want to give up?
   B Yes, I bite my nails. I just can't stop and I'm a teacher, so I have to hide my hands from the kids because I don't want to set a bad example.

CD1 48 see page 33

CD1 49 see page 33

CD1 50

Conversation 1
A Hello, it's me again. I just remembered that I have a doctor's appointment in the morning. Could we possibly make it lunch instead of coffee?
B Um … no problem. I can do lunch, too. How about 12:30 in the usual restaurant?

Conversation 2
A Would you mind if we didn't go out to eat after work? I want to watch the game on TV.
B Hey, we could have dinner at Morgan's. They have a huge screen. We could both watch the game there.
A You're on. Great idea!

Conversation 3
A So, anyway, there I was just finishing my report, when suddenly the boss calls me into his office and he starts going on about my performance …
B Sorry, darling, I really do want to hear all about it, but the baby's crying. Do you think you could go and check him? He might need a new diaper.

Conversation 4
A Help! Ugh … I don't know what's wrong with my computer. The screen's frozen again.
B I'll try and fix it if you like. I'm pretty good with computers.
A Go ahead. Be my guest. I've had it with this machine!

UNIT 5

CD2 2 Things our grandchildren may never see

H = Hannah   D = Dan
H Do you ever worry about what the world will be like when our grandchildren grow up?
D Hold on! We haven't had our baby yet. I'm not thinking about grandchildren!
H I know, but having a baby makes me wonder— what will the world be like when he or she grows up? Look at these pictures. Don't they make you worry about what could happen in the future?
D Mmm—OK, of course things are going to change a lot in the next hundred years, even in the next fifty, but …
H I know, and I'm getting worried. Everyone says global warming is a fact nowadays. No one says it *may* get warmer or it *might* get warmer anymore. Scientists say that it definitely *will* get warmer. It's going to be a very different world for our children and grandchildren.
D Look, Hannah, it's no good worrying. Not *all* scientists think the same …
H Yes, I know, but *most* do. It says here over 2,500 climate scientists agree. They say temperatures might rise by up to 39°F before the end of the century. Dan, this is the world our son or daughter is going to grow up in.
D Hannah, you have to take it easy. You're having a baby soon and …
H I can't help being worried. If the Arctic ice melts, there'll be floods, and the polar bears will have nowhere to live. Oh, and look at this …
D Come on, Hannah. Look here, it also says humans are clever enough to find solutions. We'll do our part, and we'll bring up our baby to do the same. Every little bit helps …
H OK, but maybe it won't help. It may be too late already.

CD2 3
1. A Do you think the earth will continue to get warmer?
   B Yes, I do. The more I read about it, the more I think it will. A few years ago I wasn't so sure.
2. A Do you think all the ice will melt at the Poles?
   B Well, I don't think *all* the ice will melt, but a lot has melted already. Do you know a new island near Greenland has just appeared? They thought it was part of the mainland, but it was just an ice bridge and it melted. It's called Warming Island. A good name, don't you think?
3. A Do you think Polar bears will become extinct?
   B I think they might. They only live in the Arctic, and I read that the ice there has decreased by 14% since the 1970s.
4. A Do you think more people will travel by train?
   B Definitely. I think lots more people will choose train travel when they can, especially across Europe. Of course it won't always be possible.
5. A Do you think that air travel will be banned to reduce CO₂ emissions?
   B Well, I think it could become much more expensive to travel by air, but I don't think it'll be banned.
6. A Do you think new sources of energy will be found?
   B I hope so. Some people say nuclear energy is the only answer, but I think this could cause more problems. Actually, I like wind farms. They look amazing. But I know some people hate them.
7. A Do you think there'll be more droughts or floods in the world?
   B I don't really know. There might be both droughts and floods. I think parts of New York City may be flooded, including most of the lower Manhattan shoreline.
8. A Do you think our lifestyles will have to change?
   B Definitely. They're already changing. We're told all the time to do things like drive smaller cars, use cleaner gas, and recycle our trash. That worries me a lot—the amount of trash we make.

CD2 4 Discussing grammar
1. A Have you decided about your vacation yet?
   B No, not yet. We've never been to Costa Rica, so we might go there.
2. A Are you going to take an umbrella?
   B No, I'm not. The forecast says it'll be fine all day.
3. A Why are you making a list?
   B Because I'm going shopping. Is there anything you want?
4. A Would you like to go out to dinner tonight?
   B Sorry, I'm working late. How about tomorrow night? I'll call you.
5. A What are you doing Saturday night?
   B I'm not sure yet. I may go to a friend's, or she may come here.
6. A Are you enjoying your job more now?
   B No, I'm not. I'm going to look for another one.
7. A Your team's no good! It's 2 to nothing Brazil!
   B Come on. It's only half-time. I think they could still win.
8. A You won't pass your exams next month if you go out every night.
   B I know, I'll study harder. I promise.

CD2 5
1. **Thailand**
A prolonged period of heavy rain and thunderstorms will affect parts of the country on Friday and into Saturday. Rainfall could total 1 to 2 inches in the south, but there may be up to 2 to 4 inches in the north. The heavy rain might lead to flooding in some areas.

2. **Canada**
High winds following in the path of Hurricane Gloria will head north from the U.S. overnight. They could reach up to 100 miles per hour and may cause damage to buildings across northwest Ontario. These winds are going to bring with them high temperatures across the country and thunderstorms in many areas.

3. **The U.S.**
The country's heatwave is going to continue. Temperatures could rise to more than 100 degrees Fahrenheit by midday tomorrow. New York City's mayor is going to send out teams of workers to distribute 22,000 bottles of drinking water to local people. Meteorologists say that temperatures will continue to rise until the end of the week.

4. **Mexico**
Tropical storm Barbara is forming rapidly off the coast and will move towards land. Winds of 68 miles per hour are expected, and they could reach the popular resort of Acapulco over the next few days. Hotels and houses may have to be evacuated. Meteorologists say that the winds might even reach hurricane status.

5. **South Africa**
For the first time in 25 years forecasters in Johannesburg are predicting snow. Up to 4 inches could fall during the night, and this is causing much excitement throughout the city. SABC News is reporting that some parents are going to take their children to the local parks after midnight to play in the snow. Tambo International Airport may be affected.

CD2 6
1. I think it'll be a cold night tonight. Wear warm clothes if you go out.
2. I think I'll get a new computer. I want a laptop this time.
3. I think I'll take a cooking class. I can't even boil an egg.
4. I think you'll like the movie. It's a great story and really well cast.
5. I think we'll get to the airport in time. But we'd better get moving.
6. I think you'll get the job. You have all the right qualifications.

CD2 7
1. I don't think it'll be a cold night tonight. You won't need to take a jacket.
2. I don't think I'll get a new computer. It may seem old-fashioned to you, but it's OK for me.
3. I don't think I'll take a cooking class. I'll get lessons from my mom.
4. I don't think you'll like the movie. It's not really your kind of thing.

119 Audio Scripts

5. I don't think we'll get to the airport in time. There's too much traffic.
6. I don't think you'll get the job. You're too young, and you have no experience.

CD2 8 Rocket man
I = Interviewer   S = Steve

I Steve Bennett's ambition was to be a rocket scientist. A few years ago, he almost won a $16 million prize, the X prize. Now Steve's building a rocket that will take him and two passengers up into space. He believes that space tourism is not really that far away.
S Space tourism is just about to happen. There are a lot of people around the world who are actually putting a lot of money into space tourism. It's simply a question of *when*, not *if*. You know, just as the Internet made billionaires, well, space tourism is going to make trillionaires. And all the big names are at it—you have Jeff Bezos, he did Amazon.com, he's building his own spaceship; you have Richard Branson, even he is commissioning someone to build a spaceship for him. So it really is going to happen.
I And what are you intending to take people into space in? What is your rocket?
S A rocket that can carry three people into space. We're not going into orbit. It's going straight up and straight down, but it will go into space. It'll give you about three or four minutes of weightlessness, you'll see the blackness of space, the curvature of the earth, and you really will become an astronaut just like the early American astronauts.
I And you are going to be one of the people who goes up, so it's going to be you and two space tourists. Have you been up in this exact rocket before, Steve?
S No, we're still working on this one. We've launched about 16 big rockets to date but this actual space rocket, called *Thunderstar*, we're still working on it, we're still building it. I was influenced as a small child watching too many episodes of "Thunderbirds," I think.
I Were you very much struck by the first moon landings as well?
S Yup. I was about five years old when they landed on the moon. Um, my parents wouldn't let me stay up to watch the actual landing, which was a shame.
I How mean!
S Yeah … yeah. Well, they just didn't get it. "Oh, it's marvelous, but they should spend the money on something better" kind of attitude.
I Lots of young boys will have had exactly that kind of experience themselves, but very few of them will now have a business that's making rockets and thinking about taking people up into space. Did you always feel you eventually would get to do it professionally?
S I kept it pretty quiet. Ten, fifteen years ago you start talking about space tourism and people, they think you're nuts, so you keep that kind of thing to yourself.
I Why do we really need to do that, though? I mean, is there actually any necessity to have more humans in space?
S Well, that's pretty much where the human race needs to be in terms of expansion. You know, there's enough resources in space to allow the human race to grow and expand for the next 10 thousand years.
I What kind of training do you have to do in order to go up in the rocket?
S Actually, one of the most important things we do is skydiving training. We feel that if you don't have what it takes to jump out of an airplane with a parachute, you really shouldn't be strapping yourself to the top of a 17-ton rocket.

I These two other people who've already booked their place on your *Thunderstar*, do you know who they are?
S Absolutely. I've taken their money.
I Right.
S Well, it's a couple. It's two people who want to fly in space. They came to me a few years ago and basically they said, "Steve, we want to fly in the rocket. Here's the money." They gave me half a million dollars for it.
I And how often do you consider the possibility that something might go wrong?
S I think about it every day, you know? I've built a lot of rockets, most of them have worked really well. Some haven't, and I think about that every day.

CD2 9 Spoken English
1. A Did your team win?
   B No, but they did pretty well.
2. A You haven't lost your cell phone again!
   B No, no. I'm pretty sure it's in my bag somewhere.
3. A Do you enjoy skiing?
   B I do, but I'm pretty hopeless at it.
4. A What do you think of my English?
   B I think it's pretty good.

CD2 10 see page 103

CD2 11
1. Carlos and Diana don't get along at all. They disagree about everything.
2. Money does not always lead to happiness.
3. My aunt says today's kids are all rude and impolite.
4. Thanks for your advice, it was really helpful. I really appreciate your kindness.
5. My dad is useless at fixing his computer. I always have to help him.
6. Please don't misunderstand me. I didn't mean to be unkind. I'm really sorry.
7. Timmy fell off his bike and hit his head. He was unconscious for a few hours.
8. What was your wife's reaction when she heard you'd won the lottery?

CD2 12 see page 40

CD2 13
1. A The doctors are going to operate on my grandma's knee.
   B Oh, no!
   A Don't worry, it's not a serious operation.
2. A Did you explain the homework to Maria?
   B I did, but I don't think she understood my explanation.
3. A I couldn't find the book I wanted in the library.
   B Did you ask the librarian? She'll tell you if they have it.
4. A Can I have a copy of that photograph?
   B Yes, of course. I'm not a great photographer, but this one's OK, isn't it?
   A It is. Usually I can't stand photos of me.

CD2 14 Arranging to meet
G = Gary   M = Mike

G Mike, it's me, Gary.
M Gary! Long time no see. How are you doing?
G Good, thanks. Listen, I'm coming up next weekend, and I was wondering if we could meet.
M I'd love to, but this weekend of all weekends, I am *so* busy.
G Look, you must have some free time.
M Yeah, I'll get my calendar. Hold on … OK … shoot!
G Right. What are you doing Friday evening?

M Friday evening? Um … that's my Spanish class. Our company's going to do a lot of work in Mexico, so we're all learning Spanish. But I finish work early on Friday. I could meet you in the afternoon.
G No, I'm afraid that's no good. My train doesn't get in until 7 o'clock. Do you have any free time on Saturday?
M Um … let me see. What about Saturday afternoon? I'm having my hair cut in the morning and then I'm meeting my sister for lunch, but I'm free in the afternoon.
G Oh, no, sorry, Saturday afternoon, I can't. I have an appointment with a real estate agent. I'm going to look at one of those amazing new apartments by the river. Didn't I tell you? I'm changing jobs and moving back to the big city.
M Hey, great news, Gary. I knew small town life wasn't your thing!
G So, what about Saturday evening? Is Saturday evening any good?
M Sorry, the evening's out for me. I'm going to the theater with friends. We've had it booked forever. But … hold on, what time are you leaving on Sunday?
G Late morning. I'm taking the 11:55 train.
M Hey, I have a good idea. Why don't we meet at the station?
G Good idea, we could have coffee together.
M I have an even better idea. They make great pancakes at the cafe. Let's meet there for breakfast. How about ten o'clock?
G Sounds good to me. But can you make it 10:30? It *is* Sunday.
M Fine. 10:30 it is. I'll see you then. Bye, Gary! Hope you like the apartment.
G Fingers crossed. Bye, Mike. See you Sunday.

CD2 15
1. I was wondering if we could meet.
2. I could meet you in the afternoon.
3. What about Saturday afternoon?
4. Is Saturday evening any good?
5. Why don't we meet at the station?
6. Let's meet there for breakfast.
7. How about ten o'clock?
8. Can you make it 10:30?

UNIT 6

CD2 16 see page 42

CD2 17 Describing places
1. What's your apartment like?
   It's modern, but it's cozy.
2. How big is it?
   About 850 square feet.
3. How many rooms are there?
   There are three rooms.
4. What size is the kitchen?
   Nine feet by eight.
5. Which floor is it on?
   The fourth.
6. Which part of town is it in?
   It's south of the river.
7. How far is it to the stores?
   Just five minutes.

CD2 18 Describing things
1. What brand is it?
   Sony.
2. How much does it weigh?
   3 pounds.
3. What's it made of?
   Carbon and titanium.

Audio Scripts 120

4. What's this button for?
 It turns it on.
5. How big is the screen?
 13.2 inches.
6. How long is the battery life?
 Eight hours.
7. What size is the hard disk?
 80 gigabytes.

CD2 19
1. What kind of bread do you have?
2. What flavor ice cream would you like?
3. Which way do we go?
4. What brand is your camera?
5. What kind of food do you like?
6. Whose top are you wearing?
7. How long does it take to get to the airport?
8. How far is your house from the beach?
9. How often do you go to the movies?
10. How many of you want coffee?
11. What size shoes do you wear?

CD2 20
fresh fruit
latest fashions
pretty woman
clear sky
fast food
crowded restaurant
casual clothes
close friend
handsome man
straight hair
cozy room
challenging job

CD2 21
1. Peter and I lived together in college.
2. He's a good student. He tries hard.
3. A Where's the town hall?
 B Go straight ahead.
4. Say that again. I didn't hear you.
5. Don't talk so loud! Everyone can hear you.
6. Why do you drive so fast? Slow down!
7. His wife's name is Mariana, not Maria! Get it right.
8. The vacation was a disaster. Everything went wrong.
9. This room is cool, even in summer.
10. A Are you ready?
 B Almost. Give me another five minutes.

CD2 22 My most treasured possession
1. Amy
I would have to save my photo albums. They have all the photos of my kids, when they were babies, their first steps, you know, when they walked for the first time, their birthday parties, their first day at school. And all the holidays we spent together. All those memories are irreplaceable.

2. Jack
I know it sounds a little sad, but I would have to save my computer. Not very sentimental, but very practical. It has all my work, all my e-mail contacts, several thousand photos, address books, work calendar for the next year. I just couldn't live without it.

3. Lucy
I have a matching hairbrush and hand mirror that belonged to my grandmother. She was given them as a wedding present, and she gave them to me before she died. I don't use them, but they're always on the shelf in my bedroom, and every time I see them I think of her. They're solid silver, and they're pretty heavy. They're not especially nice, but they have immense sentimental value.

CD2 23
Jen
The person that I'm closest to in my family is probably my mother. She's the kind of person you can talk to about anything. She's very open, my mother, and I can talk to her about boyfriends, stuff that's bothering me at work, friendships, anything. We have our ups and downs, of course, but basically we have an easy relationship. We go shopping together. What I like about her is her attitude. She's young at heart, like me, not old-fashioned or anything like that.

Brett
I'm closest to my grandmother. Um, my father I don't really get along with. We don't really see eye to eye on anything. My mother I hardly ever see. She's too busy. My grandmother and I like doing the same things. Um … we like watching TV and having lunch together. We love playing cards. And I think emotionally I'm closer to her than I am to my parents … because she and I have a similar attitude to life. I think we both like people. We're very outgoing, sociable, and open.

Julia
The person I'm closest to in my family, I think, would be my father. We stay up late listening to music and talking a lot. What I like about him is that he's interesting and interested. He has a curiosity about life. We can talk about anything and everything. We have the same sense of humor, the same love of life. My friends all love him because he's so funny. He doesn't care what people think of him, and I guess that's great. He's pretty cool, my dad.

Susan
I think the person that I'm probably closest to is my sister. The thing I love about her is the way everyone knows her. It doesn't matter where we go, everyone says, "Hi, Sarah! How you doin'?" I'm just her little sister. People call me "Baby Sarah," but that's fine. We're so different. We have big fights. She's so hyperactive and loud, she can't sit still, she has to have people around her, and everyone loves her. In many ways she drives me crazy. She just can't think straight. Me, I'm a lot quieter. I'm happy on my own. But we're so proud of each other.

Chris
I'm closest to my twin, Nick. Obviously, we have so much in common. The same friends. The same soccer team. The same music. We go everywhere together. But we have crazy arguments about everything. We're like oil and water. I'm like my Mom—calm and easygoing. Nick's like my Dad— very bad-tempered. They fight like cats and dogs. But things have changed now that we're older. We appreciate each other more. The biggest difference is probably interests. I'm into all things history and politics, and Nick's interested in science and nature. But of course we're a lot closer than just brothers and sisters. In a way we're like one. I would trust him like I would trust no one else.

CD2 24 In a department store
1. A Morning!
 B Hello. I'd like to try on these shoes, please.
 A Certainly, sir. What size do you wear?
 B Nine. That's 41, isn't it?
 A Uh, no, I think you'll find 43 would be more comfortable, sir.
2. A Do you have these soccer shorts for age 10-11?
 B I'm afraid that's all we have. We're sold out of that size.
 A Will you be getting any more in?
 B We should be getting a delivery by the end of the week.
3. A Do you have any sofas like this in stock?
 B No, we don't. They all have to be ordered.
 A How long does delivery take?
 B It all depends, but on average about eight weeks.
4. A Yes?
 B I'd like this fruit bowl, please.
 A Certainly. Is it a present?
 B Yes, it is.
 A Would you like me to gift wrap it?
 B Ooh, that would be great! Thank you so much!
5. A I like this.
 B How does it feel?
 A I love the color, but the size is wrong. It doesn't fit me. It's too tight.
 B Too bad. It really suits you. What's it made of?
 B Cashmere. It's so soft.
6. A Yes, sir?
 B I'll have this coffee maker, please.
 A Certainly. Do you have a store card?
 B No, just a debit card.
 A That's fine. Pin number, please. Keep your receipt. That's your warranty.
 B How long is the warranty for?
 A For a year.

Grammar Reference

UNIT 1

1.1 Tenses

Unit 1 aims to review what you know. It has examples of the Present Simple and Continuous, the Past Simple and Continuous, and the Present Perfect. There are also examples of the passive voice. All these forms are covered again in later units.

Present tenses	Unit 2
Past tenses	Unit 3
Present Perfect	Unit 7
Passive	Units 2, 3, 7

1.2 Verbs

1. There are three classes of verbs in English.

   Auxiliary verbs *do*, *be*, and *have*
   These are used to form tenses, and to show forms such as questions and negatives.

   Modal auxiliary verbs
   Must, can, should, might, will, and *would* are examples of modal auxiliary verbs. They "help" other verbs, but unlike *do, be,* and *have,* they have their own meanings. For example, *must* expresses obligation; *can* expresses ability. (See Units 4, 5, 9, 11.)

   Full verbs
   These are **all** the other verbs in the language, for example, *play, run, help, think, want, go, see, eat, enjoy, live, die, swim,* etc.

2. *Do, be,* and *have* can also be used as full verbs with their own meanings.

   do
   I **do** my laundry on Saturdays.
   She **does** a lot of business in Latin America.

   be
   We **are** in class at the moment.
   They **were** at home yesterday.

   have
   He **has** a lot of problems.
   They **have** three children.

3. There are two forms of *have* in the present.

   have as a full verb
   I **have** a job.
   Do you **have** an apartment?
   He doesn't **have** a car.

1.3 Auxiliary verbs and tenses

1 *be* and the continuous forms

Be + verb + *-ing* is used to make continuous verb forms which describe activities in progress and temporary activities.
He**'s washing** his hair. (Present Continuous)
They **were going** to work. (Past Continuous)
I**'ve been learning** English for two years. (Present Perfect Continuous)
I'd like **to be lying** on the beach right now. (Continuous infinitive)

2 *be* and the passive voice

Be + past participle is used to form the passive.
Paper **is made** from wood. (Present Simple passive)
My car **was stolen** yesterday. (Past Simple passive)
The house **has been** redecorated. (Present Perfect passive)
This homework needs **to be done** tonight. (Passive infinitive)
There is an introduction to the passive on page 131.

3 *have* and the perfect forms

Have + past participle is used to make perfect verb forms.
He **has worked** in seven different countries. (Present Perfect)
She was crying because she **had had** some bad news. (Past Perfect)
I'd like **to have met** Napoleon. (Perfect infinitive)
Perfect means "completed before," so Present Perfect means "completed before now." Past Perfect means "completed before a time in the past."

1.4 Auxiliary verbs and negatives

1. To make a negative, add *-n't* to the auxiliary verb. If there is no auxiliary verb, use *don't/doesn't/didn't*.

Positive	Negative
He's working.	He **isn't** working.
I was thinking.	I **wasn't** thinking.
We've seen the play.	We **haven't** seen the play.
She works in a bank.	She **doesn't** work in a bank.
They like skiing.	They **don't** like skiing.
He went on vacation.	He **didn't** go on vacation.

2. It is possible to contract the auxiliaries *be* and *have* and use the uncontracted *not*.
   He's **not** playing today. (= He **isn't** playing today.)
   We're **not** going to Italy after all. (= We **aren't** going to Italy …)
   I've **not** read that book yet. (= I **haven't** read that book yet.)
   BUT   I**'m not** working.   NOT   ~~I amn't working~~.

1.5 Auxiliary verbs and questions

1. To make a question, invert the subject and the auxiliary verb. If there is no auxiliary verb, use *do/does/did*.

Question	
She's wearing jeans.	What **is she** wearing?
You were born in Mexico.	Where **were you** born?
Peter's been to China.	**Has Peter** been to China?
I know you.	**Do I** know you?
He wants ice cream.	What **does he** want?
They didn't go out.	Why **didn't they** go out?

2. There is usually no *do/does/did* in subject questions.
   Who wants ice cream?   What flavor ice cream **do** you want?
   What happened to your eye? What **did** you do to your eye?
   Who broke the window?   How **did** you break the window?

1.6 Auxiliary verbs and short answers

Short answers are very common in spoken English. If you just say *Yes* or *No*, it can sound rude. To make a short answer, repeat the auxiliary verb. In the Present and Past Simple, use *do/does/did*.

Short answer
Are you coming with us?   **Yes,** I **am.**
Have you had breakfast?   **No,** I **haven't.**
Does she like walking?   **No,** she **doesn't.**
Did Mary call?   **Yes,** she **did.**

Grammar Reference   129

UNIT 2

2.1 Present Simple

Form
The form is the same for *I/we/you/they*.
*I **work** from 9–5 P.M.*
*They **don't work** full time.*
*Where **do** you **work**?*

He/She/It: add *-s* or *-es*, and use *does/doesn't* in questions and short answers.
*He **doesn't work** on weekends.*
*Where **does** she **live**?*

Short answer
Do you live in Chicago?   Yes, **we do**.
Does he have a car?   No, **he doesn't**.

Use
The Present Simple is used to express:
1. an action that happens again and again (a habit).
   *I **go** to work by car.*
   *She **drinks** ten cups of coffee a day.*
2. a fact that is always true.
   *Ronaldo **comes** from Brazil.*
   *My daughter **has** brown eyes.*
3. a fact that is true for a long time (a state).
   *He **works** in a bank.*
   *I **live** in an apartment near downtown.*

Spelling of *he/she/it* forms
1. Most verbs add *-s* to the base form of the verb.
   wan**ts**   ea**ts**   help**s**   drive**s**
2. Add *-es* to verbs that end in *-ss*, *-sh*, *-ch*, *-x*, and *-o*.
   kisse**s**   washe**s**   watche**s**   fixe**s**   goe**s**
3. Verbs that end in a consonant + *-y* change the *-y* to *-ies*.
   carr**ies**   fl**ies**   worr**ies**   tr**ies**
   But verbs that end in a vowel + *-y* only add *-s*.
   buy**s**   say**s**   play**s**   enjoy**s**

2.2 Adverbs of frequency

1. We often use adverbs of frequency with the Present Simple.

   0% ─────────── 50% ─────────── 100%
   never rarely hardly ever not often sometimes often usually always

2. They go before the main verb, but after the verb *to be*.
   *I **usually** start at 9:00.*   *They're **usually** here by now.*
   *I **rarely** see Peter these days.*   *We're **rarely** home on weekends.*
3. *Sometimes* and *usually* can also go at the beginning or the end.
   ***Sometimes** we play cards.*   *We play cards **sometimes**.*
   ***Usually** I go shopping with friends.*   *I go shopping with friends **usually**.*

2.3 Present Continuous

Form
am/is/are + verb + *-ing*
*I'**m playing** tennis.*
*He'**s cooking** lunch.*
*I'**m not enjoying** my new job.*
*They **aren't working** today.*
*What'**s** he **doing**?*
*Where **are** you **living**?*

Short answer
Are you going by train?   **Yes, I am./No, I'm not.**

Use
The Present Continuous is used to express:
1. an activity that is happening now.
   *Don't turn the TV off. I'**m watching** it.*
   *You can't speak to Lisa. She'**s taking** a bath.*
2. an activity that is not necessarily happening at the moment of speaking but is happening around now.
   *Don't take that book. Jane'**s reading** it.*
   *I'**m taking** a Spanish evening class this year.*
3. a temporary activity.
   *Peter is a student, but he'**s working** as a waiter during the summer.*
   *I'**m living** with friends until I find a place of my own.*
4. a planned future arrangement.
   *I'**m having** lunch with Glenda tomorrow.*
   *We'**re meeting** at 1:00 outside the restaurant.*

Spelling of verb + *-ing*
1. Most verbs add *-ing* to the base form of the verb.
   go**ing**   wear**ing**   visit**ing**   eat**ing**
2. Verbs that end in one *-e* lose the *-e*.
   smoking   coming   hoping   writing
   BUT   lie → lying
   Verbs that end in *-ee* don't drop an *-e*.
   agreeing   seeing
3. Verbs of one syllable, with one vowel and one consonant, double the consonant.
   sto**pp**ing   ge**tt**ing   ru**nn**ing   pla**nn**ing   jo**gg**ing
   If the final consonant is *-y* or *-w*, it is not doubled.
   playing   showing

2.4 State verbs

1. There are certain groups of verbs that are usually only used in the Present Simple. Their meanings are related to states or conditions that are facts, not activities.

Verbs of thinking and opinions

believe	think	understand	suppose	expect	agree
doubt	know	remember	forget	promise	mean
imagine	realize	deserve	guess		

*I **believe** you.*
*Do you **understand** what I mean?*
*I **know** his face, but I **forget** his name.*

Verbs of emotions and feelings

| like | love | hate | care | hope |
| wish | want | prefer | adore | dislike |

*I **like** black coffee.*
*Do you **want** to go out?*
*I **don't care**.*

Verbs of having and being

| belong | own | have | possess | contain | cost | seem |
| matter | need | depend | weigh | resemble | fit | involve |

*This book **belongs** to Jane.*
*How much **does** it **cost**?*
*He **has** a lot of money.*

Verbs of the senses

| look | hear | taste | smell | feel | sound |

*The food **smells** good.*
*My hair **feels** soft.*

We often use *can* when the subject is a person.
*I **can** hear someone crying.*
***Can** you smell something burning?*

2. Some of these verbs can be used in the Present Continuous, but with a change of meaning. In the continuous, the verb expresses an activity, not a state. Compare:

*I **think** you're right.* (opinion)	*We're **thinking** of going to the movies.* (mental activity)
*He **has** a lot of money.* (possession)	*She's **having** a bad day.* (activity)
*I **see** what you mean.* (= understand)	*Are you **seeing** Dan tomorrow?* (activity)
*The soup **tastes** awful.* (state)	*I'm **tasting** the soup to see if it needs salt.* (activity)

2.5 THE PASSIVE

Form

to be + past participle

The tense of the verb *to be* changes to give different tenses in the passive.
*Are you **being served**?* (Present Continuous)
*My car **is insured** with ASM.* (Present Simple)
*Were you **taken** to visit the museum?* (Past Simple)
*I've **been invited** to a wedding.* (Present Perfect)
*I'd love **to be introduced** to a movie star.* (Passive infinitive)

Use

1. Passive sentences move the focus from the subject to the object of active sentences.
   *Shakespeare **wrote** Hamlet in 1601 while he was living in London.*
   *Hamlet, the most famous play in English literature, **was written** by William Shakespeare.*
   The passive is not another way of expressing the same sentence in the active. We choose the active or the passive depending on what we are more interested in.

2. *By* and the agent are often omitted in passive sentences if …
   … the agent is not known:
   *I **was robbed** last night.*
   … the agent is not important:
   *This bridge **was built** in 1886.*
   … the agent is obvious:
   *I **was fined** $100 for speeding.*

3. The passive is associated with an impersonal, formal style. It is often used in notices and announcements.
   *Customers **are requested** to refrain from eating in the store.*
   *It **has been noticed** that reference books **have been removed** from the library.*

4. In informal language, we often use *you*, *we*, and *they* to refer to people in general or to no person in particular. In this way, we can avoid using the passive.
   *You **can buy** stamps in many places, not just post offices.*
   *They're **building** a new department store downtown.*
   *We **speak** English in this shop.*

❗ Many past participles are used as adjectives.
*I'm very **interested** in modern art.*
*We were extremely **worried** about you.*
*I'm **exhausted**! I've been working hard all day.*

2.6 Present Simple and Present Continuous passive

Form

Present Simple Passive (*am/is/are* + past participle)
*Most workers **are paid** monthly.*
***Is** the tip **included** in the check?*

Present Continuous Passive (*am/is/are being* + past participle)
*This road **is being widened**.*
*Are you **being served**?*

Use

The uses are the same in the passive as in the active.
*My car **is serviced** every six months.* (habit)
*Computers **are used** everywhere.* (fact that is always true)
*The house **is being redecorated** right now.* (activity happening now)

UNIT 3

3.1 PAST TENSES

We use different past tenses to describe moments and periods of time in the past.
Look at the diagram. Read the sentences.
When Andrea arrived at work at 9:00 …

———— 8:30 ———— **9:00** ———— 9:30 ———— 10:00 ————

*… her secretary **had opened** the mail.*

*… her secretary **was opening** the mail.*

*… her secretary **opened** the mail.*

3.2 Past Simple

Form

The form of the Past Simple is the same for all persons.
*He **left** at three o'clock.*
*They **arrived** three weeks ago.*
*She **didn't finish** on time yesterday.*
*I **didn't visit** my parents last weekend.*
*When **did** he **finish** the report?*
*What time **did** his train **leave**?*

Short answer

Did you enjoy the meal?   **Yes**, we **did**./**No**, we **didn't**.

Use

The Past Simple is used to express:

1. a finished action in the past.
   *We **met** in 2000.*
   *I **went** to Boston last week.*
   *John **left** two minutes ago.*

2. actions that follow each other in a story.
   *Mary **walked** into the room and **stopped**. She **listened** carefully. She **heard** a noise coming from behind the curtain. She **threw** the curtain open, and then she **saw** …*

3. a past situation or habit.
   *When I **was** a child, we lived in a small house by the sea. Every day I **walked** for miles on the beach with my dog.*
   This use is often expressed with *used to*. See 3.5 on page 132.
   *We **used to** live in a small house … I **used to** walk for miles …*

Grammar Reference   131

Spelling of verb + -ed

1. Most regular verbs add -ed to the base form of the verb.
   worked   wanted   helped   washed
2. When the verb ends in *-e*, add *-d*.
   liked   used   hated   cared
3. If the verb has only one syllable, with one vowel + one consonant, double the consonant before adding *-ed*.
   stopped   planned   robbed
   But we write *cooked*, *seated*, and *moaned* because there are two vowels.
4. The consonant is not doubled if it is *-y* or *-w*.
   played   showed
5. In most two-syllable verbs, the end consonant is doubled if the stress is on the second syllable.
   pre'ferred   ad'mitted
   But we write *'entered* and *'visited* because the stress is on the first syllable.
6. Verbs that end in a consonant + *-y* change the *-y* to *-ied*.
   carried   hurried   buried
   But we write *enjoyed*, because it ends in a vowel + *-y*.

There are many common irregular verbs.

▶▶ **Irregular verbs page 155**

Past Simple and time expressions

Look at the time expressions that are common with the Past Simple.

I met her	last night.
	two days ago.
	yesterday morning.
	in 2001.
	in the summer.
	when I was young.

3.3 Past Continuous

Form

was/were + verb + -ing

*I **was learning** Japanese.*
*They **were driving** to Tokyo.*
*We **weren't waiting** for a long time.*
*What **were** they **doing**?*
*Where **was** he **studying**?*

Short answer

Were you looking for me?   *Yes, I **was**./No, I **wasn't**.*
Were they waiting outside?   *Yes, they **were**./No, they **weren't**.*

Use

The Past Continuous is used:

1. to express activities in progress before, and probably after, a particular time in the past.
   *At seven o'clock this morning I **was having** my breakfast.*
   *You made a lot of noise last night. What **were** you **doing**?*
2. for descriptions.
   *Jan looked beautiful. She **was wearing** a green cotton dress. Her eyes **were shining** in the light of the candles that **were burning** nearby.*
3. to express an interrupted past activity.
   *When the phone rang, I **was taking** a shower.*
   *While we **were playing** tennis, it started to rain.*
4. to express an incomplete activity.
   *I **was reading** a book during the flight. (I didn't finish it.)*
   *I **watched** a movie during the flight. (the whole movie)*

3.4 Past Simple or Past Continuous?

1. Sometimes both tenses are possible. The Past Simple focuses on past actions as complete facts. The Past Continuous focuses on the duration of past activities. Compare:
   A *I didn't see you at the party last night.*
   B *No. I **stayed** at home and **watched** the game.*
   A *I didn't see you at the party last night.*
   B *No, I **was watching** the game at home.*
2. Questions in the Past Simple and Past Continuous refer to different time periods. The Past Continuous asks about activities before; the Past Simple asks about what happened after.
   A *What **were** you **doing** when the accident happened?*
   B *I **was shopping**.*
   A *What **did** you **do** when you saw the accident?*
   B *I **called** the police.*

3.5 used to

Used to expresses a habit or state in the past that is now finished.
*I **used to** read comics when I was a kid. (but I don't now)*
*My dad and I **used to** play basketball together. (but we don't now)*
***Did** you **use to** read comics when you were a child?*
*This town **didn't use to** be a nice place to live, but then it changed.*

3.6 Past Perfect

Perfect means "completed before." The Past Perfect refers to an action in the past that was completed before another action in the past.

Form

The form of the Past Perfect is the same for all persons.

Positive and negative

I	'd (had)	seen him before.
You	hadn't	finished work at six o'clock.
We		

Question

| Where had | you
she
they | been before? |

Short answer

Had he already left?   *Yes, he **had**./No, he **hadn't**.*

Use

1. The Past Perfect is used to make clear that one action in the past happened *before* another action in the past.
   *When I got home, I found that someone **had broken** into my apartment and **had stolen** my DVD player.*
   *I didn't go to the movie theater because I'd **seen** the movie before.*
2. The Past Simple tells a story in chronological order.
   Sue met Pete in college. They dated for six years. They got married last month.
   The Past Perfect can be used to tell a story in a different order.
   Sue and Pete got married last month. They'd met in college and had dated for six years.
3. Notice the difference between these sentences.
   *When I got to the party, Peter **went** home.*
   (= First I arrived, then Peter left.)
   *When I got to the party, Peter **had gone** home.*
   (= First Peter left, then I arrived.)

132 Grammar Reference

4. The Past Perfect Continuous refers to longer actions or repeated activities.
   We were exhausted because we'd been driving all day.

3.7 Past tenses in the passive

Form
Past Simple Passive: *was/were* + past participle
The museum was opened in 1987.
We were robbed last night.

Past Continuous Passive: *was/were being* + past participle
The vase was being restored.

Past Perfect Passive: *had been* + past participle
The house had been redecorated.

Use
The uses are the same in the passive as in the active.
The bridge was built in 1876. (finished action in the past)
The bomb was being defused when it exploded. (interrupted past activity)
The letter didn't arrive because it had been sent to my old address. (one action before another action in the past)

UNIT 4

4.1 have to

Form
has/have + to + infinitive
You have to go to school.
She has to study hard.

He doesn't have to wear a uniform.
We don't have to take exams.

Does she have to study math?
Do they have to leave now?

Use
1. *Have to* expresses strong obligation.
   You have to work hard if you want to succeed.
2. *Have to* expresses a general obligation based on a law or rule, or based on the authority of another person.
   Children have to go to school until they are 16.
   Mom says you have to clean your room before you go out.
3. *Have to* is impersonal. It doesn't necessarily express the opinion of the speaker.
   The doctor says I have to lose weight.
   People all over the world have to learn English.
4. *Have to* has all verb forms. *Must* doesn't.
   I had to work last night. (Past)
   You'll have to study hard. (Future)
   She's rich. She's never had to do any work. (Present Perfect)
   I hate having to get up on winter mornings. (-ing form)

4.2 have got to

1. *Have got to* is common in spoken English. It is more informal than *have to*.
   I've got to go now. See you!
   We've got to get up early tomorrow.

2. *Have got to* expresses an obligation now, or on a particular occasion soon.
   I've got to stop eating ice cream! It's too yummy!
   You've got to pay me back tomorrow.

3. *Have to* expresses a general repeated obligation.
   I always have to tell my parents where I'm going.
   Teachers have to prepare lessons and correct homework.

4.3 MODAL AND RELATED VERBS

These are the modal verbs:
can, could, may, might, will, would, should, must, ought to.
They are used before other verbs and add meanings, such as certainty, possibility, obligation, ability, and permission.
You must be exhausted.
I can swim.
It might rain.

Form
1. There is no *-s* in the third person singular.
   She can ski. He must be tired. It might rain.
2. There is no *do/does/don't/doesn't* in the question or negative.
   What should I do?   Can I help you?   You mustn't steal!
   He can't dance.   I won't be a minute.
3. Modal auxiliary verbs are followed by the infinitive without *to*. The exception is *ought to*.
   You must go.   I'll help you.   You ought to see a doctor.
4. They have no infinitives and no *-ing* forms. Other expressions are used instead.
   I'd love to be able to ski.
   I hate having to get up on cold winter mornings.
5. They don't usually have past forms. Instead, we use them with Perfect infinitives.
   You should have told me that you can't swim. You might have drowned!
   Or we use other expressions.
   I had to study hard in school.
6. *Could* is used with a past meaning to talk about a general ability.
   I could swim when I was six. (= general ability)

   To talk about ability on one specific occasion, we use *was able to/ managed to*.
   The prisoner was able to/managed to escape by climbing onto the roof of the prison.

Use
1. Modal verbs express our attitudes, opinions, and judgments of events. Compare:
   "Who's that knocking on the door?"
   "It's John." (This is a fact.)
   "Who's that knocking on the door?"
   "It could/may/might/must/should/can't/'ll be John." (These all express our attitude or opinion.)
2. Each modal verb has at least two meanings. One use of all of them is to express possibility or probability. (See Units 5 and 11.)
   I must mail this letter! (= obligation)
   You must be tired! (= deduction, probability)

   Could you help me? (= request)
   We could go to Thailand for our vacation. (= possibility)

   You may go home now. (= permission)
   "Where's Anna?"   "I'm not sure. She may be at work." (= possibility)

Grammar Reference 133

4.4 Obligation: *should*, *ought to*, and *must*

Should, *ought to*, and *must* are modal verbs. See 4.3 on page 133 for form.

Use

1. *Should* and *ought to* express mild obligation, suggestions, or advice. They express what, in the speaker's opinion, is the right or best thing to do. We often use them with *I think/don't think …*
   *You're always asking me for money. I think you **should** spend less.*
   *You **shouldn't** sit so close to the television! It's bad for your eyes.*
   *You **ought to** be more careful with your money.*

2. We often use *Do you think …?* in the question.
   ***Do you think** I should see a doctor?*
   *What **do you think** I should wear to the party?*

3. *Must*, like *have to*, expresses strong obligation. *Must* can express an obligation that involves the speaker's opinion. It is personal.
   *I **must** pass the exam to graduate.*
   *The government **must** do something about the environment.*

4. *Must* is also associated with a formal, written style.
   *All visitors **must** show proper ID.*
   *Books **must** be returned on or before the due date.*

have to and must

1. *Have to* and *must* are sometimes interchangeable.
   *I **must** be home by midnight.*
   *I **have to** be home by midnight.*

2. There is sometimes a difference in meaning. *Must* usually expresses the feelings and wishes of the speaker.
   *I **must** buy my mother a birthday card.*
   *Tommy, you **must** look after your toys.*

   Have to often expresses an obligation that comes from somewhere else.
   *You **have to** work hard in this life.*
   *Visitors **have to** report to reception.*

   It is for this reason that you need to be careful when you say *You must …*, because you can sound authoritarian.

   Have to is used more than *must*. If you don't know which to use, use *have to*.

3. Question forms with *have to* are more common.
   *Do I **have to** do what you say?*
   Must I …? is unusual.

🔴 Remember, *have to* has all verb forms. *Must* can only refer to present or future time when used to express obligation.

don't have to

1. *Don't have to* expresses absence of obligation — you can, but it isn't necessary.
   *Some people iron their socks, but you **don't have to**. I think it's a waste of time.*
   *When you go into a store, you **don't have to** buy something. You can just look.*

4.5 Permission: *can* and *be allowed to*

Can is a modal verb. See 4.3 on page 133 for form.

Use

The main use of *can* is to express ability.
*I **can** swim.*
Can and *be allowed to* express permission. *Can* is more informal and usually spoken.
*You **can** borrow my bike, but you **can't** have the car. I need it.*
*They **can't** come in here with those muddy shoes!*
*You're **allowed to** get married when you're 18.*
*Are we **allowed to** use a dictionary for this test?*

4.6 Making requests: *can*, *could*, *will*, and *would*

1. There are many ways of making requests in English.
   ***Can** I speak to you, please?*
   ***Could** I ask you a question?*
   ***Will** you help me, please?*
   ***Would** you pass me the salt?*

   ***Would** you mind passing me the water?*
   ***Do you mind if** I open the window?*
   ***Would you mind if** I closed the window?*
   Can, *could*, *will*, and *would* are all modal verbs.

2. *Could* is a little more formal; *can* is a little more familiar. *Could I …?* and *Could you …?* are very useful because they can be used in many different situations.
   ***Could** I try on this sweater?*
   ***Could** you tell me the time?*

3. Here are some ways of responding to requests:
   A *Excuse me! Could you help me?*
   B *Sure./Of course./Well, I'm afraid I'm a little busy right now.*
   A *Would you mind if I opened the window?*
   B *No, not at all./No, that's fine./Well, I'm a little cold, actually.*

4.7 Making offers: *will* and *should*

1. The contracted form of *will* is used to express an intention, decision, or offer.
   *Come over after work. **I'll** cook dinner.*
   *"It's Jane's birthday today."   "Is it? **I'll** buy her some flowers."*
   *Dave**'ll** give you a lift.*
   *Give it back or we**'ll** call the police!*

2. We use *should* to make an informal suggestion.
   *"What **should** we have for dinner?"*
   *"Where **should** we go?"*

134 Grammar Reference

UNIT 5

5.1 FUTURE FORMS

1. There is no future tense in English. Instead, English has several forms that can refer to the future.
   I'll see you later. (*will*)
   We're going to see a movie tonight. (*going to*)
   I'm seeing the doctor tomorrow. (Present Continuous)
   If the traffic's bad, I *might be* late. (*might*)
   Who knows? You *may win*! (*may*)
   Take an umbrella. It *could rain* later. (*could*)

2. The difference between them is not about near or distant future, or certainty. The speaker chooses a future form depending on how he/she sees the future event. Is it a plan, a decision, an intention, an offer, an arrangement, or a prediction?

5.2 *will/going to* and the Present Continuous

Form
Positive and negative
I'll see you later.
I *won't be* late.
We're going to stay in a hotel.
We *aren't going to rent* a beach house.
I'm meeting Jan for lunch.
I'm not seeing her till 2:00.

Question
When *will* you *be* back?
Where *are* you *going to stay*?
What time *are* you *seeing* Jan?

❗ We avoid saying *going to come* or *going to go*.
We're coming tomorrow.
When *are* you *going* home?

Facts and predictions
will

1. The most common use of *will* is as an auxiliary verb to show future time. It expresses a future fact or prediction. It is called the pure future or the Future Simple.
   We'll be away for two weeks.
   Those flowers *won't grow* under the tree. It's too dark.
   Our love *will last* forever.
   You'll be sick if you eat all those sweets!

2. *Will* for a prediction can be based more on an opinion than a fact.
   I don't think Laura *will do* very well on her exam. She doesn't do any work.
   I am convinced that inflation *will fall* to three per cent next year.

going to

1. *Going to* can also express a prediction, especially when it is based on a present fact. There is evidence now that something is certain to happen.
   She's *going to have* a baby.
   (We can see she's pregnant.)
   Our team *is going to win* the game.
   (It's the fourth quarter, and there are only five minutes left to play.)
   It *isn't going to rain* today.
   (Look at that beautiful blue sky.)

2. Sometimes there is no difference between *will* and *going to*.
   This government *will ruin* the country.
   This government *is going to ruin* the country.

Plans, decisions, intentions, and arrangements
will
Will is used to express a decision, intention, or offer made at the moment of speaking.

I'll have the steak, please.	NOT ~~I have the steak …~~
Give me a call. *We'll* go out for coffee.	NOT ~~We go …~~
There's the phone! *I'll* get it.	NOT ~~I get …~~

going to
Going to is used to express a future plan, decision, or intention made before the moment of speaking.
When I grow up, *I'm going to be* a doctor.
Jane and Peter *are going to get married* after they graduate.
We're going to paint this room blue.

Arrangements

1. The Present Continuous can be used to express a future arrangement between people. It usually refers to the near future.
   We're going out with Jeremy tonight.
   I'm having my hair cut tomorrow.
   What *are* we *having* for lunch?

2. Think of the things you put in your calendar to remind you of what you are doing over the next few days and weeks. These are the kinds of events that are expressed by the Present Continuous for the future. There is often movement or activity.
   I'm meeting Peter tonight.
   The Taylors *are coming* for dinner.
   I'm seeing the doctor in the morning.

3. You can't use the Present Simple for this use.

We're going to a party on Saturday night.	NOT ~~We go …~~
I'm having lunch with Sarah.	NOT ~~I have …~~
What are you doing this evening?	NOT ~~What do you do …~~

4. Sometimes there is no difference between an arrangement and an intention.
   We're going to get married in the spring.
   We're getting married in the spring.

5.3 Future possibility: *may/might/could*

Form
May, *might*, and *could* are modal verbs.

Positive and negative

I	may might could	see you later.		I	may not might not	get the job.

Question
Questions about future possibility are often asked with *Do you think … will …?*
Do you think you'll get the job?

Use

1. *May*, *might*, and *could* all express a future possibility.

It	may might could	rain later.

2. *May* can be more formal.
   The government *may* increase income tax.

3. *Could* suggests something less definite.
   I *could* be a champion if I trained hard.
   The house is nice, but it *could* be beautiful.

Grammar Reference 135

UNIT 6

6.1 Information questions

1. *What* and *which* can be followed by a noun.
   What color are your eyes?
   What size shoes do you wear?
   What sort of music do you like?
   Which part of town do you live in?
   Which way do we go?
   Which one do you want?

   We use *which* when there is a limited choice.
   Which one do you want, the red one or the blue one?
   Which restaurant should we go to?

   We use *what* when there is (almost) unlimited choice.
   What language do they speak in Brazil?
   What car do you drive?

   Sometimes there is no difference.
   What/Which newspaper do you read?
   What/Which channel is the game on?

2. *Whose* can be followed by a noun.
   Whose book is this?
   Whose is this book?

3. *How* can be followed by an adjective or an adverb.
   How tall are you?
   How big is the memory?
   How far is it to the station?
   How often do you go to the movies?
   How long does it take you to get ready?

4. *How* can be followed by *much* or *many*.
   How many rooms are there?
   How much money do you have?

6.2 What ... like? How ...?

1. *What ... like?* asks about the permanent nature of people and things. It asks for a general description.
   What's Mexican food **like**?   Really tasty.
   What's Pete **like**?   He's a great guy.

2. *How ...?* asks about the present condition of something. This condition can change.
   How's work these days?   It's better than last year.
   How was the traffic this morning?   It was worse than usual.

   To ask about the weather, we can use both questions.
   How's the weather | where you are?
   What's the weather like |

3. *How ...?* asks about people's health and happiness.
   How's Peter?   He's fine.

4. *How ...?* asks about people's reactions and feelings.
   How's your meal?
   How's your new job?

6.3 Relative clauses

1. Relative clauses identify which person or thing we are talking about. They make it possible to give more information about the person or thing.
   The boy went to the beach. (Which boy?)
   The boy **who lives next door** went to the beach.
   The book is very good. (Which book?)
   The book **that I bought yesterday** is very good.
   There is a photo of the hotel. (Which hotel?)
   There is a photo of the hotel **where we stayed**.

2. We use *who/that* to refer to people, and *which/that* to refer to things.
   This book is about a girl **who marries a millionaire**.
   What was the name of the horse **that won the race**?

3. When *who* or *that* is the object of a relative clause, it can be left out.
   The person **you need to talk to** is on vacation.
   The movie **I watched last night** was very good.
   But when *who* or *that* is the subject of a relative clause it must be included.
   I like people **who are kind and considerate**.
   I want a computer **that's easy to use**.

4. *Which* can be used to refer to the whole previous sentence or idea.
   I passed my driving test on the first attempt, **which was a surprise**.
   Jane can't come to the party, **which is a shame**.

5. We use *whose* to refer to someone's possessions.
   That's the man **whose wife won the lottery**.
   That's the woman **whose dog ran away**.

6. We can use *where* to refer to places.
   The hotel **where we stayed** was right on the beach.
   We went back to the place **where we first met**.

6.4 Participles

Participles after a noun define and identify in the same way as relative clauses.
That woman **driving** the red Porsche is my aunt.
The men **seen** outside were probably the thieves.

Extra Materials

UNIT 1 page 9

EVERYDAY ENGLISH
Role play

4 Work with a partner. Act out the situations.

1. You are with an American friend when you meet another friend. Introduce them to each other.

2. You are in a coffee shop. You asked for a latte and a muffin, but the waiter has brought you an espresso and a piece of chocolate cake.

3. You are in a hotel. You call reception because the television in your room isn't working.

4. You are at the airport and you can't find the check-in desk for your flight to Bangkok. Ask at the information desk.

5. You are cooking for some friends. They're all hanging out in the living room and chatting. You want them to come to the table and help themselves to the food.

CD1 13 Listen and compare.

UNIT 2 page 13

4 Work in small groups. Look at the chart. Compare the correct answers with your ideas.

Which salaries do you think are unfair? Are any surprising?

Who earns how much in the U.S.?	
Doctor	$140,000
Basketball player	$1 million
Senior Director	$750,000
Nurse	$25,000
Supermarket cashier	$20,000
Pilot	$65,000
Police officer	$30,000
Teacher	$40,000
Lawyer	$200,000
Farmer	$48,000

Extra Materials   143

UNIT 3 *page 22*

READING – A Shakespearean tragedy

5 Read Shakespeare's lines from *Romeo and Juliet* in more modern English.

Romeo AND Juliet

1 **Tybalt** Peace? I hate the word peace like I hate hell, all Montagues, and you.

2 **Romeo** Did my heart ever love before now? Because I never saw true beauty before tonight.

Juliet The only man I love is the son of the only man I hate!

3 **Juliet** Oh, Romeo, Romeo, why are you a Montague? Forget your father and give up your name. … What's a Montague anyway? … A rose would smell just as sweet if it was called any other name.

4 **Romeo** I have fallen in love with the beautiful daughter of rich Capulet.

Friar Laurence This marriage may be lucky enough to turn the hatred between your families into pure love.

5 **Romeo** Now, Tybalt, … Mercutio's soul is above our heads. Either you, or I, or both of us have to join him.

Tybalt You, wretched boy, are going with him now.

6 **Friar Laurence** Take this small bottle and drink the liquid. No pulse or breath will show you are alive for forty-two hours.

Juliet Give it to me! Love will give me strength.

7 **Juliet** Romeo, Romeo, Romeo! Here's a drink. I drink to you.

Nurse Oh, hateful day! There has never been so black a day as today. Oh, painful day!

8 **Romeo** Eyes, look for the last time! Arms, make your last embrace! … Here's to my love! Oh, honest pharmacist! Your drugs work quickly. So I die with a kiss.

9 **Juliet** What's this here? A cup, closed in my true love's hand? Poison, I see … I will kiss your lips. Some poison is still on your lips. Your lips are warm. Oh, happy dagger! Let me die!

10 **Prince** There never was a more tragic story than the story of Juliet and her Romeo.

UNIT 4 page 26

MODERN DILEMMAS

Readers ask, readers reply

2 Read the readers' questions and the complete replies.

1 A reader asks

How should I deal with my difficult and disagreeable neighbor? He is in the habit of dumping his garden waste along the public sidewalk between our two houses.
Jim T. via e-mail

(d) A reader replies

You have to act with self-control in a situation like this. I don't think you should confront him. Arguments between neighbors can get out of hand. If I were you, I'd quietly clean up his mess and keep the peace.

2 A reader asks

Is it OK to greet people with a "How are you?" In California (my home) it's considered friendly, but here in New York some people react with a cold look. Should I be less friendly in my greetings?
Erica Fleckberg, New York

(c) A reader replies

You don't have to be like New Yorkers just because you're in New York. Be yourself. Be warm. Be Californian.

3 A reader asks

My new PC automatically picks up wireless networks to gain access to the Internet. This includes the one belonging to my neighbor. Is it right for me to use it?
Richard Dalton, via e-mail

(g) A reader replies

You can stop others from accessing your wireless network if you use a password. You must tell your neighbor this. It's the only right thing to do.

4 A reader asks

My stepfather's driver's license was suspended for six months for speeding, but we have learned that he still drives over the speed limit all the time. Should we keep quiet or inform the police?
Stella Milne, Connecticut

(a) A reader replies

Your stepfather is not allowed to drive by law. He is a danger to himself and everyone else on the road. You must call "Crimestoppers" and report him. You don't have to give your name.

5 A reader asks

I am a medical student. After I graduate in June, I have one month before my first house job starts. My fiancée says that I am not allowed to claim unemployment benefits for this month. I disagree, because I'll be unemployed. The benefits are for all those who are out of work. What do you think?
J. R. Collin, via e-mail

(b) A reader replies

Your fiancée's right. You aren't allowed to claim unemployment benefits, but I think you are allowed other benefits. You should check online. Perhaps you should claim these benefits and give the money to charity, if you don't need it.

6 A reader asks

Is it wrong for me to record CDs borrowed from my local library? I am not denying anyone the money, as I wouldn't buy the CD anyway.
Pete Rodriguez, via e-mail

(e) A reader replies

It's not only wrong, it's illegal. You are not allowed to do this. You should buy the CD.

7 A reader asks

Is it ever permissible to lie to children? I lied to my two-year-old granddaughter to remove her from a fairground ride without a tantrum. I said: "You must get off now because the man is going to get his dinner." She got down without a fuss. But I'm worried that if she remembers this, she won't trust me in the future.
Barbara Hope, Philadelphia

(f) A reader replies

Not only should you lie sometimes, you often have to. Children should be treated with respect, but you don't have to explain everything. Also, it's a good way to learn that we often have to tell "white lies," such as when asked, "What do you think of my new boyfriend?" "Um—very nice."

Extra Materials

UNIT 4 page 29

LISTENING AND SPEAKING
Rules for life

4 Work with a partner. Read the song and discuss which word fits best in each of the blanks.

I Believe
by Ian Dury & the Blockheads

I believe in _____ _____	*bottle banks / Citibank
And beauty from within	
I believe in saying _____	hello / thanks
And fresh _____ on the skin	hair / air
I believe in healthy _____	walks / thoughts
As tonic for the feet	
I believe in serious talks	
And _____ _____ to eat	just enough / a lot
Chorus	
That's what I believe	
Surprising as it seems	
I believe that happiness	
Is well within our dreams	
I believe in being _____	nice / polite
In spite of what you think	
I believe in good _____	manners / advice
And not too much to _____	eat / drink
I believe in being _____	faithful / true
In everything you try to _____	do / say
I believe in me and you	
I hope you share my _____	point of view / opinion
Chorus	
I believe in being _____	generous / kind
Especially when it's hard	
I believe an open _____	mind / door
Can show a fine regard	
I believe that _____ make	manners / kindness
A person good to know	
I believe in birthday _____	presents / cake
And going _____	in the snow / with the flow
Chorus	
That's what I believe	
Although it seems naïve	
I believe that _____	happiness / peace and love
Are there to be achieved	
That's what I believe . . .	

*Recycling bin

CD1 46 Listen and check.

Word List

Here is a list of most of the new words in the units of *American Headway* Student Book 3.

adj = adjective
adv = adverb
conj = conjunction
coll = colloquial
n = noun
opp = opposite

pl = plural
prep = preposition
pron = pronoun
pp = past participle
v = verb

UNIT 1

archaeology n /arki'alədʒi/
area n /'ɛriə/
background n /'bækgraʊnd/
barrel n /'bærəl/
Basque adj /bæsk/
beat v /bit/
bilingual adj /ˌbaɪ'lɪŋgwəl/
block n /blak/
brief v /brif/
bright adj /braɪt/
cancellation n /kænsə'leɪʃn/
cherish v /'tʃɛrɪʃ/
client n /'klaɪənt/
close-knit adj /kloʊsnɪt/
communal adj /kə'myunl/
community n /kə'myunəti/
cosmopolitan adj /ˌkazmə'palətn/
cracked adj /krækd/
culture n /'kʌltʃər/
daylight n /'deɪlaɪt/
demolition n /ˌdɛmə'lɪʃn/
destroy v /dɪ'strɔɪ/
dressmaker n /'drɛsmeɪkər/
earthquake n /'ərθkweɪk/
elderly adj /'ɛldərli/
end up v /ˌɛnd ʌp/
equator n /ɪ'kweɪtər/
extended family n /ɪk'stɛndɪd 'fæmli/
extinct adj /ɪk'stɪŋkt/
fee n /fi/
filling n /'fɪlɪŋ/
for good /fər gʊd/
forbid v /fər'bɪd/
frail adj /freɪl/
frugally adv /'frugəli/
global warming n /gloʊbl wɔrmɪŋ/
(not) go far /goʊ far/
go live v /goʊ lɪv/
go on about v /goʊ an ə'baʊt/
a great deal /eɪ greɪt dil/
headquarters n /'hɛdkwɔrtərz/
heritage n /'hɛrətɪdʒ/
hold v /hoʊld/
hopefully adv /'hoʊpfli/
hospitality n /ˌhaspə'tæləti/
iceberg n /'aɪsbərg/
immediate family n /ɪ'midiət 'fæmli/
kit n /kɪt/
life expectancy v n /laɪf ɪk'spɛktənsi/

make v /meɪk/
means n /minz/
motto n /'matoʊ/
muffin n /'mʌfən/
municipal adj /my'nɪsəpl/
neutral adj /'nutrəl/
nonsense n /'nansɛns/
noticeable adj /'noʊtəsəbl/
on the clock n /an ðə klak/
operator n /'apəreɪtər/
performance n /pə'fɔrməns/
pin number n /'pɪn nʌmbər/
policy n /'paləsi/
preschool n /'priskul/
prestigious adj /prɛ'stɪdʒəs/
presumably adv /prɪ'zuməbli/
profile n /'proʊfaɪl/
propaganda n /prapə'gændə/
provide v /prə'vaɪd/
pyjamas n /pə'dʒæməz/
raise v /reɪz/
reach v /ritʃ/
regret n /rɪ'grɛt/
research n /'risərtʃ/
settle down v /'sɛtl daʊn/
shortly adv /'ʃɔrtli/
similarity n /ˌsɪmə'lærəti/
slum n /slʌm/
storey n /'stɔri/
stressed adj /strɛst/
structure n /'strʌktʃər/
stuck adj /stʌk/
suburb n /'sʌbərb/
survey n /sər'veɪ/
take home v /teɪk hoʊm/
take out v /teɪk aʊt/
tricky adj /'trɪki/
ultimately adv /'ʌltəmətli/
urgent adj /'ərdʒənt/
vote n/v /voʊt/
well-balanced adj /wɛl'bælənst/
widely adv /'waɪdli/

UNIT 2

accomplish v /ə'kamplɪʃ/
actually adv /'æktʃuəli/
amazing adj /ə'meɪzɪŋ/
ambassador n /æm'bæsədər/
annual adj /'ænyuəl/
attend v /ə'tɛnd/
bake v /beɪk/
baking dish n /beɪkɪŋ dɪʃ/

banking n /'bæŋkɪŋ/
bargain n /'bargən/
be in touch /bi ɪn tʌtʃ/
(surf)board n /sərfbɔrd/
boarding school n /bɔrdɪŋ skul/
boil v /bɔɪl/
broadcaster n /'brɔdkæstər/
budget n /'bʌdʒət/
butler n /'bʌtlər/
buzz n /bʌz/
cash flow n /'kæʃ floʊ/
cashier n /kæ'ʃɪər/
catch up on phr v /kætʃ ʌp an/
challenging adj /'tʃælənʤɪŋ/
charity n /'tʃærəti/
charming adj /'tʃarmɪŋ/
check n /tʃɛk/
chop v /tʃap/
concentrate v /'kansntreɪt/
concerned adj /kən'sərnd/
conservative adj /kən'sərvətɪv/
convenient adj /kən'vinyənt/
cope v /koʊp/
day off n /deɪ ɔf/
decent adj /'disənt/
deputy n /'dɛpyəti/
documentary n /ˌdakyə'mɛntəri/
drill n /drɪl/
dutiful adj /'dutɪfl/
duty n /'duti/
earn a living /ˌərn eɪ 'lɪvɪŋ/
earner n /'ərnər/
eccentric adj /ɪk'sɛntrɪk/
employee n /ɛm'plɔɪi/
engagement n /ɪn'geɪdʒmənt/
enormous adj /ɪ'nɔrməs/
expand v /ɪk'spænd/
extensively adv /ɪk'stɛnsɪvli/
extravagantly adv /ɪk'strævəgəntli/
ferry n /'fɛri/
fly by v /'flaɪ ˌbaɪ/
food processor n /ˌfud 'prasɛsər/
frustration n /frʌ'streɪʃn/
fry v /fraɪ/
get away from it all v /ˌgɛt ə'weɪ frəm ɪt ɔl/
goods pl n /gʊdz/
ground beef n /ˌgraʊnd bif/
handyman n /'hændimæn/
hardware n /'hardwɛr/
hard-working adj /ˌhard 'wərkɪŋ/
head of state n /ˌhɛd əv 'steɪt/
heir n /ɛr/
helmet n /'hɛlmət/

herb n /ərb/
honey n /'hʌni/
host v /hoʊst/
housekeeper n /'haʊskipər/
huge adj /hyudʒ/
human resources n /ˌhyumən 'risɔrsɪz/
hunting n /'hʌntɪŋ/
in charge /ɪn tʃardʒ/
in response to /ɪn rɪ'spans tə/
include v /ɪn'klud/
inconvenience adj /ˌɪnkən'vinyəns/
industry n /'ɪndəstri/
invoice n /'ɪn vɔɪs/
involve v /ɪn'valv/
land v /lænd/
laptop n /'læptap/
lavish adj /'lævɪʃ/
lifeguard n /'laɪfgard/
lifetime n /'laɪftaɪm/
lively adj /'laɪvli/
madly adv /'mædli/
maid n /meɪd/
managing director n /ˌmænɪdʒɪŋ də'rɛktər/
manufacture v /ˌmænyə'fæktʃər/
meditate v /'mɛdəteɪt/
memo n /'mɛmoʊ/
mild adj /maɪld/
mix v /mɪks/
modernize v /'madərnaɪz/
monarch n /'manərk/
negotiate v /nə'goʊʃieɪt/
occupy v /'akyəpaɪ/
organic adj /ɔr'gænɪk/
payment n /'peɪmənt/
peel v /pil/
personnel n /ˌpərsə'nɛl/
plant v /plænt/
politician n /palə'tɪʃn/
porter n /'pɔrtər/
portray v /pɔr'treɪ/
praise v /preɪz/
product n /'pradʌkt/
promote v /prə'moʊt/
qualification n /ˌkwaləfə'keɪʃn/
racket n /'rækət/
reception n /rɪ'sɛpʃn/
reckon v /'rɛkən/
recruit v /rɪ'krut/
redecorate v /ri'dɛkəreɪt/
ridiculous adj /rɪ'dɪkyələs/
roast v /roʊst/

Word List 148

sales *pl n* /seɪlz/
screwdriver *n* /ˈskrudraɪvər/
serve an *ace v* /sərv ən ˈeɪs/
shift *n* /ʃɪft/
shooting *n* /ˈʃutɪŋ/
situate *v* /ˈsɪtʃueɪt/
sketch *v* /skɛtʃ/
small talk *n* /ˈsmɔl tɔk/
soap *n* /soʊp/
socializer *n* /ˈsoʊʃlaɪzər/
stay fit *v* /steɪ fɪt/
squeeze *v* /skwiz/
state *n* /steɪt/
stiff *adj* /stɪf/
support *v* /səˈpɔrt/
sweat *v* /swɛt/
sweetheart *n* /ˈswithɑrt/
tackle *v* /ˈtækl/
tantrum *n* /ˈtæntrəm/
tax *n* /tæks/
tell off *v* /ˌtɛl ɔf/
throne *n* /θroʊn/
trade *n* /treɪd/
training *n* /ˈtreɪnɪŋ/
understanding *n* /ˌʌndərˈstændɪŋ/
valet *n* /væˈleɪ/
VIP *n* /vi aɪ pi/
weed *v* /wid/
weigh *v* /weɪ/
well intentioned *adj* /wɛl ɪnˈtɛnʃnd/
workforce *n* /ˈwɔrkfɔrs/
zoom *n* /zum/

UNIT 3

according to *prep* /əˈkɔrdɪŋ tə/
alliance *n* /əˈlaɪəns/
apothecary *n* /əˈpɑθɪkɛri/
art dealer *n* /ɑrt ˈdilər/
asylum *n* /əˈsaɪləm/
ban *v* /bæn/
banish *v* /ˈbænɪʃ/
beg *v* /bɛg/
beloved *adj* /bɪˈlʌvd/
blind *adj* /blaɪnd/
bury *v* /ˈbɛri/
cemetery *n* /ˈsɛmətɛri/
clumsy *adj* /ˈklʌmzi/
collection *n* /kəˈlɛkʃn/
comfort *v* /ˈkʌmfərt/
commit *v* /kəˈmɪt/
dagger *n* /ˈdægər/
dawn *n* /dɔn/
declare *v* /dɪˈklɛr/
decline *v* /dɪˈklaɪn/
depression *n* /dɪˈprɛʃn/
despite *prep* /dɪˈspaɪt/
dismiss *v* /dɪsˈmɪs/
donate *v* /ˈdoʊneɪt/
dynasty *n* /ˈdaɪnəsti/
electric *adj* /ɪˈlɛktrɪk/
embrace *n* /ɪmˈbreɪs/
enemy *n* /ˈɛnəmi/
entire *adj* /ɪnˈtaɪər/
eternal *adj* /ɪˈtərnl/

exile *v* /ˈɛksaɪl/
explode *v* /ɪkˈsploʊd/
fair *adj* /fɛr/
fair enough *adj* /fɛr ɪˈnʌf/
fall in love *v* /fɔl ɪn lʌv/
farewell *n* /fɛrˈwɛl/
fellow *adj* /ˈfɛloʊ/
feud *n* /fyud/
fiercely *adv* /fɪrsli/
friar *n* /fraɪər/
funny *adj* /ˈfʌni/
genius *n* /ˈdʒinyəs/
glad *adj* /glæd/
go out *v* /goʊ ˈaʊt/
go weak at the knees /goʊ wik ət ðə niz/
grief *n* /grif/
hateful *adj* /ˈheɪtfll/
hatred *n* /ˈheɪtrəd/
(fall) head over heels /hɛd oʊvər ˈhilz/
heavily *adv* /ˈhɛvili/
horrible *adj* /ˈhɔrəbl/
horrified *adj* /ˈhɔrəfaɪd/
identify *v* /aɪˈdɛntəfaɪ/
insane *adj* /ɪnˈseɪn/
lifeless *adj* /ˈlaɪfləs/
liquor *n* /ˈlɪkə(r)/
madness *n* /ˈmædnəs/
move *v* /muv/
nature *n* /ˈneɪtʃər/
nightmare *n* /ˈnaɪtmɛr/
nobleman *n* /ˈnoʊblmən/
on the mend /ɑn ðə mɛnd/
overwhelmed *adj* /oʊvərˈwɛlmd/
pay attention /ˌpeɪ əˈtɛnʃn/
peace *n* /pis/
pleasurable *adj* /ˈplɛʒərəbl/
poison *n* /ˈpɔɪzn/
porcelain *n* /ˈpɔrsəlɪn/
precious *adj* /ˈprɛʃəs/
pretend *v* /prɪˈtɛnd/
priceless *adj* /ˈpraɪsləs/
psychiatrist *n* /saɪˈkaɪətrɪst/
psychology *n* /saɪˈkɑlədʒi/
publish *v* /ˈpʌblɪʃ/
pulse *n* /pʌls/
quarrel *v* /ˈkwɔrəl/
rancour *n* /ˈræŋkə(r)/
razor blade *n* /ˈreɪzər ˌbleɪd/
reciprocated *adj* /rɪˈsɪprəkeɪtɪd/
recognize *v* /ˈrɛkəgnaɪz/
regrettable *adj* /rɪˈgrɛtəbl/
reject *v* /rɪˈdʒɛkt/
rescue *v* /ˈrɛskyu/
sense of humor *n* /sɛns əv ˈhyumər/
a shame /eɪ ʃeɪm/
shiny *adj* /ˈʃaɪni/
slip *v* /slɪp/
slow motion *n* /sloʊ ˈmoʊʃn/
soul *n* /soʊl/
stab *v* /stæb/
stuff *n* /stʌf/
stunned *adj* /stʌnd/
suicide *n* /ˈsuəsaɪd/
swear *v* /swɛr/

tension *n* /ˈtɛnʃn/
testify *v* /ˈtɛstəfaɪ/
tight *adj* /taɪt/
tomb *n* /tum/
tragedy *n* /ˈtrædʒədi/
tragic *adj* /ˈtrædʒɪk/
treasure *n* /ˈtrɛʒər/
unfortunate *adj* /ʌnˈfɔrtʃənət/
uninvited *adj* /ˌʌnɪnˈvaɪtəd/
unite *v* /yuˈnaɪt/
unrecognized *adj* /ʌnˈrɛkəgnaɪzd/
upside down *adj* /ˌʌpsaɪd daʊn/
valuable *adj* /ˈvælyəbl/
vase *n* /veɪs/
vial *n* /ˈvaɪəl/
voluntarily *adv* /ˈvɑləntɛrɪli/
warring *adj* /ˈwɔrɪŋ/
wed *v* /wɛd/
weep *v* /wip/
windowsill *n* /ˈwɪndoʊsɪl/
woe *n* /woʊ/
wretched *adj* /ˈrɛtʃəd/
yoga *n* /ˈyoʊgə/

UNIT 4

access *n* /ˈæksɛs/
accessory *n* /əkˈsɛsəri/
adjust *v* /əˈdʒʌst/
apparently *adv* /əˈpærəntli/
appreciate *v* /əˈpriʃieɪt/
bargain *n* /ˈbɑrgən/
battered *adj* /ˈbætərd/
benefit *n* /ˈbɛnəfɪt/
borrow *v* /ˈbɑroʊ/
bottle bank *n* /ˈbɑtl bæŋk/
bring up *v* /ˌbrɪŋ ˈʌp/
chore *n* /tʃɔr/
claim *v* /kleɪm/
code *n* /koʊd/
confront *v* /kənˈfrʌnt/
consider *v* /kənˈsɪdər/
council house *n* /ˈkaʊnsl ˌhaʊs/
cut off *v* /ˌkʌt ˈɔf/
deal with *v* /dil wɪð/
decorate *v* /ˈdɛkəreɪt/
demand *n* /dɪˈmænd/
dig *v* /dɪg/
dilemma *n* /dəˈlɛmə/
disagreeable *adj* /ˈdɪsəˈgriəbl/
discipline *n* /ˈdɪsəplɪn/
disqualify *v* /dɪsˈkwɑləfaɪ/
domestic *adj* /dəˈmɛstɪk/
dump *v* /dʌmp/
electronic *adj* /ɪlɛkˈtrɑnɪk/
enter *v* /ˈɛntər/
equipment *n* /ɪˈkwɪpmənt/
era *n* /ˈɪrə/
fair *adj* /fɛr/
fiancée *n* /fiˈɑnseɪ/
freeze *v* /friz/
gadget *n* /ˈgædʒət/
gain *v* /geɪn/
get through *v* /ˌgɛt θru/
gift-wrap *v* /gɪft-ræp/
give in *v* /ˌgɪv ˈɪn/

go with the flow /goʊ wɪð ðə floʊ/
great-grandmother *n* /greɪt ˈgrænmʌðər/
greet *v* /grit/
hi-tech *adj* /ˌhaɪ-tɛk/
in spite of *prep* /ɪnˈspaɪt əv/
iron *v* /ˈaɪərn/
keep quiet *v* /kip kwaɪət/
lift *n* /lɪft/
make *n* /meɪk/
match *n* /mætʃ/
medical *adj* /ˈmɛdɪkl/
menace *n* /ˈmɛnəs/
military service *n* /ˈmɪlətɛri ˈsərvəs/
missionary *n* /ˈmɪʃənɛri/
morals *pl n* /ˈmɔrəlz/
naïve *adj* /nɑˈiv/
open *adj* /ˈoʊpən/
optimist *n* /ˈɑptəmɪst/
out of work /ˌaʊt əv ˈwərk/
permissible *adj* /pərˈmɪsəbl/
pessimist *n* /ˈpɛsəmɪst/
pick up *v* /ˌpɪk ˈʌp/
point of view *n* /ˌpɔɪnt əv vyu/
pump *n* /pʌmp/
punk *n* /pʌŋk/
push up *v* /pʊʃ ʌp/
put up with *v* /pʊt ʌp wɪð/
qualify *v* /ˈkwɑləfaɪ/
react *v* /riˈækt/
regard *n* /rɪˈgɑrd/
remove *v* /rɪˈmuv/
retell *v* /ˌriˈtɛl/
row *n* /raʊ/
scary *adj* /ˈskɛri/
set an example /ˌsɛt ɪgˈzæmpl/
set up *v* /ˌsɛt ʌp/
share *v* /ʃɛr/
spread *v* /sprɛd/
space station *n* /ˈspeɪs ˌsteɪʃn/
stepfather *n* /ˈstɛpfɑðər)/
strict *adj* /strɪkt/
strip *v* /strɪp/
stuck *adj* /stʌk/
suit *v* /sut/
take after *v* /ˌteɪk ˈæftər/
take up *v* /ˌteɪk ˈʌp/
tear *n* /tɪr/
thrift *n* /θrɪft/
token *n* /ˈtoʊkən/
tonic *n* /ˈtɑnɪk/
transform *v* /trænsˈfɔrm/
transport *v* /trænˈspɔrt/
treat *n* /trit/
valuable *adj* /ˈvælyəbl/
Victorian *adj* /vɪkˈtɔriən/
wardrobe *n* /ˈwɔrdroʊb/
wireless *adj* /ˈwaɪərləs/
woodwork *n* /ˈwʊdwərk/

UNIT 5

addiction *n* /əˈdɪkʃn/
advance *n* /ədˈvæns/
alien *n* /ˈeɪliən/
amateur *adj* /ˈæmətʃər/
astronaut *n* /ˈæstrənɔt/
attitude *n* /ˈætətud/
awareness *n* /əˈwɛrnəs/
beyond your wildest dreams /bɪˈyɑnd yər ˌwaɪldɪst ˈdrimz/
blackness *n* /ˈblæknɛs/
breakthrough *n* /ˈbreɪkθru/
cause for concern /ˈkɔz fər kənˈsɜrn/
cell *n* /sɛl/
centenarian *n* /sɛntɪˈnɛriən/
confidently *adv* /ˈkɑnfədəntli/
confirmation *n* /kɑnfərˈmeɪʃn/
consciousness *n* /ˈkɑnʃəsnəs/
controversial *adj* /kɑntrəˈvərʃl/
cooking *n* /ˈkʊkɪŋ/
current *adj* /ˈkərənt/
curvature *n* /ˈkərvətʃər/
cyber- /ˈsaɪbər/
damage *n* /ˈdæmɪdʒ/
diseased *adj* /dɪˈzizd/
disorder *n* /dɪsˈɔrdər/
distribute *v* /dɪˈstrɪbyut/
drought *n* /draʊt/
emotion *n* /ɪˈmoʊʃn/
evacuate *v* /ɪˈvækyueɪt/
evidence *n* /ˈɛvədəns/
existence *n* /ɪgˈzɪstəns/
expand *v* /ɪkˈspænd/
expect (a baby) *v* /ɪkˈspɛkt/
expense *n* /ɪkˈspɛns/
extend *v* /ɪkˈstɛnd/
fiction *n* /ˈfɪkʃn/
fingers crossed /ˈfɪŋgərz krɔst/
flood *n* /flʌd/
forecast *n* /ˈfɔrkæst/
form *v* /fɔrm/
galaxy *n* /ˈgæləksi/
generate *v* /ˈdʒɛnəreɪt/
generation *n* /dʒɛnəˈreɪʃn/
get in *v* /ˌgɛt ˈɪn/
give birth *v* /ˌgɪv ˈbərθ/
glow *v* /gloʊ/
half-time *n* /ˌhæf ˈtaɪm/
heatwave *n* /ˈhitweɪv/
hopeless *adj* /ˈhoʊpləs/
hurricane *n* /ˈhərəkən/
infinite *adj* /ˈɪnfənət/
injection *n* /ɪnˈdʒɛkʃn/
knowledge *n* /ˈnɑlɪdʒ/
laboratory *n* /ˈlæbrətɔri/
limb *n* /lɪm/
major *adj* /ˈmeɪdʒər/
mammal *n* /ˈmæml/
mankind *n* /mænˈkaɪnd/
marvel *n* /ˈmɑrvl/
melt *v* /mɛlt/
meteorologist *n* /mitiəˈrɑlədʒɪst/
mission *n* /ˈmɪʃn/
nuclear energy *n* /ˈnukliər ˈɛnərdʒi/
orbit *n* /ˈɔrbət/
organ *n* /ˈɔrgən/
parallel *adj* /ˈpærəlɛl/
permafrost *n* /ˈpərməfrɔst/
pill *n* /pɪl/
presence *n* /ˈprɛzns/
primate *n* /ˈpraɪmeɪt/
prove *v* /pruv/
quote *n* /kwoʊt/
rainfall *n* /ˈreɪnfɔl/
rapidly *adv* /ˈræpədli/
realist *n* /ˈriəlɪst/
reassure *v* /riəˈʃʊr/
reduce *v* /rɪˈdus/
regenerate *v* /rɪˈdʒɛnəreɪt/
regrow *v* /rɪˈgroʊ/
replace *v* /rɪˈpleɪs/
research *v* /rɪˈsərtʃ/
resource *n* /ˈrisɔrs/
revulsion *n* /rɪˈvʌlʃn/
science fiction *n* /ˈsaɪəns fɪkʃn/
sensational *adj* /sɛnˈseɪʃnl/
sensor *n* /ˈsɛnsər/
sink into *v* /ˌsɪŋk ˈɪntu/
skydiving *n* /ˈskaɪdaɪvɪŋ/
snowstorm *n* /ˈsnoʊstɔrm/
spine *n* /spaɪn/
status *n* /ˈstætəs/
study *n* /ˈstʌdi/
suitable *adj* /ˈsutəbl/
supply *n* /səˈplaɪ/
take for granted /ˌteɪk fər ˈgræntəd/
task *n* /tæsk/
technical *adj* /ˈtɛknɪkl/
the norm *n* /ðə ˈnɔrm/
throughout *prep* /θruˈaʊt/
thunderstorm *n* /ˈθʌndərstɔrm/
transplantation *n* /trænsplænˈteɪʃn/
tropical *adj* /ˈtrɑpɪkl/
universe *n* /ˈyunəvərs/
vertebrate *n* /ˈvərtəbrət/
vigorous *adj* /ˈvɪgərəs/
virtual *adj* /ˈvərtʃuəl/
weightlessness *n* /ˈweɪtləsnɛs/

UNIT 6

appliance *n* /əˈplaɪəns/
associate *v* /əˈsoʊʃieɪt/
astronomy *n* /əˈstrɑnəmi/
attractive *adj* /əˈtræktɪv/
badly behaved *adj* /ˌbædli bɪˈheɪvd/
basement *n* /ˈbeɪsmənt/
battery *n* /ˈbætəri/
bomb *n* /bɑm/
bother *v* /ˈbɑðər/
brightly *adv* /ˈbraɪtli/
button *n* /ˈbʌtn/
cashmere *n* /ˈkæʒmɪr/
casual *adj* /ˈkæʒuəl/
cattle *n* /ˈkætl/
celebration *n* /sɛləˈbreɪʃn/
china *n* /ˈtʃaɪnə/
clearance *n* /ˈklɪrəns/
coach *n* /koʊtʃ/
consume *v* /kənˈsum/
cosmetics *pl n* /kɑzˈmɛtɪkz/
cozy *adj* /ˈkoʊzi/
cottage *n* /ˈkɑtɪdʒ/
crumble *v* /ˈkrʌmbl/
curiosity *n* /kyʊriˈɑsəti/
curly *adj* /ˈkərli/
dome *n* /doʊm/
dominant *adj* /ˈdɑmənənt/
drive sb crazy /ˌdraɪv sʌmbʌdi ˈkreɪzi/
emigrate *v* /ˈɛməgreɪt/
equipped *adj* /ɪˈkwɪpd/
file *n* /faɪl/
fluently *adv* /ˈfluəntli/
full-time *adj* /ˌfʊl ˈtaɪm/
fully *adv* /ˈfʊli/
garlic *n* /ˈgɑrlɪk/
get together *v* /ˌgɛt təˈgɛðər/
gigabyte *n* /ˈgɪgəbaɪt/
glassware *n* /ˈglæswɛr/
good-looking *adj* /ˌgʊdˈlʊkɪŋ/
gravitate *v* /ˈgrævəteɪt/
guarantee *n* /ˌgærənˈti/
handmade *adj* /ˌhændˈmeɪd/
handy *adj* /ˈhændi/
hard disk *n* /ˌhɑrd ˈdɪsk/
hard-working *adj* /ˌhɑrd ˈwɜːkɪŋ/
homecomings *n* /ˈhoʊmkʌmɪŋz/
housewife *n* /ˈhaʊswaɪf/
hut *n* /hʌt/
hyperactive *adj* /ˌhaɪpərˈæktɪv/
immense *adj* /ɪˈmɛns/
in tune with /ˌɪn ˈtun wɪð/
independent *adj* /ɪndɪˈpɛndənt/
ingredient *n* /ɪnˈgridiənt/
insecure *adj* /ɪnsəˈkyʊr/
irreplaceable *adj* /ˌɪrɪˈpleɪsəbl/
kitchenware *n* /ˈkɪtʃənwɛr/
lentils *pl n* /ˈlɛntlz/
like oil and vinegar /laɪk ɔɪl ənd ˈvɪnɪgər/
linen *n* /ˈlɪnɪn/
long-lasting *adj* /ˈlɔŋlæstɪŋ/
low-fat *adj* /loʊ ˈfæt/
loyalty *n* /ˈlɔɪəlti/
massage *n* /məˈsɑʒ/
medium height *n* /ˈmidiəm ˌhaɪt/
mud *n* /mʌd/
nightlife *n* /ˈnaɪtlaɪf/
orchard *n* /ˈɔrtʃərd/
painkiller *n* /ˈpeɪnkɪlə(r)/
panoramic *adj* /ˌpænəˈræmɪk/
paradise *n* /ˈpærədaɪs/
practical *adj* /ˈpræktɪkl/
premises *pl n* /ˈprɛməsəz/
pre-packed *adj* /ˌpriˈpækt/
prosecute *v* /ˈprɑsəkyut/
purchase *v* /ˈpərtʃəs/
rabbit *n* /ˈræbət/
remind *v* /rɪˈmaɪnd/
responsible *adj* /rɪˈspɑnsəbl/
restore *v* /rɪˈstɔr/
safety *n* /ˈseɪfti/
seek *v* /sik/
sell out *v* /ˌsɛl ˈaʊt/
sentimental *adj* /sɛntəˈmɛntl/
shelter *n* /ˈʃɛltər/
simply *adv* /ˈsɪmpli/
sociable *adj* /ˈsoʊʃəbl/
solid *adj* /ˈsɑləd/
staff *n* /stæf/
stationery *n* /ˈsteɪʃnɛri/
stone *n* /stoʊn/
subscribe *v* /səbˈskraɪb/
take-out *adj* /ˈteɪk-aʊt/
tempting *adj* /ˈtɛmptɪŋ/
terrace *n* /ˈtɛrəs/
think straight /ˈθɪŋk ˌstreɪt/
tiny *adj* /ˈtaɪni/
toiletries *pl n* /ˈtɔɪlətriz/
top floor *n* /tɑp ˌflɔr/
treasure *v* /ˈtrɛʒər/
turmeric *n* /ˈtʊrmərɪk/
wavy *adj* /ˈweɪvi/
wear *n* /wɛr/
wedding *n* /ˈwɛdɪŋ/
well behaved *adj* /ˌwɛl bɪˈheɪvd/
well dressed *adj* /ˌwɛl ˈdrɛst/
whisper *v* /ˈwɪspər/
young at heart /ˌyʌŋ ət ˈhɑrt/

Verb Patterns

Verbs + -ing	
adore can't stand don't mind enjoy finish imagine loathe	doing swimming cooking

Note
We often use the verb *go* + *-ing* for sports and activities.
   I **go swimming** every day.
   I **go shopping** on weekends.

Verbs + preposition + -ing	
give up look forward to succeed in think of	doing

Verbs + to + infinitive	
afford agree choose dare decide expect forget help hope learn manage mean need offer plan promise refuse seem want would hate would like would love would prefer	to do to come to cook

Notes
1. *Help* and *dare* can be used without *to*.
   We **helped clean up** the kitchen.
   They didn't **dare disagree** with him.
2. *Have to* for obligation.
   I **have to wear** a uniform.
3. *Used to* for past habits.
   I **used to exercise**, but I don't anymore.

Verbs + sb + to + infinitive		
advise allow ask beg encourage expect force help invite need order persuade remind tell want warn would like	me him them someone	to do to go to come

Note
Help can be used without *to*.
   I **helped** him **do** the dishes.

Verbs + sb + infinitive (no to)		
help let make	her us	do

Notes
1. *To* is used with *make* in the passive.
   We were **made to work** hard.
2. *Let* cannot be used in the passive. *Allowed to* is used instead.
   She was **allowed to leave**.

Verbs + -ing or to + infinitive (with little or no change in meaning)	
begin continue hate like love prefer start	doing to do

Verbs + -ing or to + infinitive (with a change in meaning)	
remember stop try	doing to do

Notes
1. I **remember mailing** the letter.
   (= I have a memory now of a past action: mailing the letter.)
   I **remembered to mail** the letter.
   (= I reminded myself to mail the letter. I didn't forget.)
2. I **stopped drinking** coffee.
   (– I gave up the habit.)
   I **stopped to drink** a coffee.
   (= I stopped doing something else in order to have a cup of coffee.)
3. I **tried to sleep**.
   (= I wanted to sleep, but it was difficult.)
   I **tried counting** sheep and **drinking** a glass of warm milk.
   (= These were possible ways of getting to sleep.)

Irregular Verbs

Base form	Past Simple	Past participle
be	was/were	been
beat	beat	beaten
become	became	become
begin	began	begun
bend	bent	bent
bite	bit	bitten
blow	blew	blown
break	broke	broken
bring	brought	brought
build	built	built
buy	bought	bought
can	could	been able
catch	caught	caught
choose	chose	chosen
come	came	come
cost	cost	cost
cut	cut	cut
dig	dug	dug
do	did	done
draw	drew	drawn
dream	dreamed	dreamed
drink	drank	drunk
drive	drove	driven
eat	ate	eaten
fall	fell	fallen
feed	fed	fed
feel	felt	felt
fight	fought	fought
find	found	found
fit	fit	fit
fly	flew	flown
forget	forgot	forgotten
forgive	forgave	forgiven
freeze	froze	frozen
get	got	got
give	gave	given
go	went	been/gone
grow	grew	grown
hang	hanged/hung	hanged/hung
have	had	had
hear	heard	heard
hide	hid	hidden
hit	hit	hit
hold	held	held
hurt	hurt	hurt
keep	kept	kept
kneel	knelt	knelt
know	knew	known
lay	laid	laid
lead	led	led
learn	learned	learned

Base form	Past Simple	Past participle
leave	left	left
lend	lent	lent
let	let	let
lie	lay	lain
light	lighted/lit	lighted/lit
lose	lost	lost
make	made	made
mean	meant	meant
meet	met	met
must	had to	had to
pay	paid	paid
put	put	put
read /rid/	read /rɛd/	read /rɛd/
ride	rode	ridden
ring	rang	rung
rise	rose	risen
run	ran	run
say	said	said
see	saw	seen
sell	sold	sold
send	sent	sent
set	set	set
shake	shook	shaken
shine	shone	shone
shoot	shot	shot
show	showed	shown
shut	shut	shut
sing	sang	sung
sink	sank	sunk
sit	sat	sat
sleep	slept	slept
slide	slid	slid
speak	spoke	spoken
spend	spent	spent
spoil	spoiled	spoiled
spread	spread	spread
stand	stood	stood
steal	stole	stolen
stick	stuck	stuck
swim	swam	swum
take	took	taken
teach	taught	taught
tear	tore	torn
tell	told	told
think	thought	thought
throw	threw	thrown
understand	understood	understood
wake	woke	woken
wear	wore	worn
win	won	won
write	wrote	written

Phonetic Symbols

Consonants

1	/p/	as in	pen	/pɛn/
2	/b/	as in	big	/bɪg/
3	/t/	as in	tea	/ti/
4	/d/	as in	do	/du/
5	/k/	as in	cat	/kæt/
6	/g/	as in	go	/goʊ/
7	/f/	as in	five	/faɪv/
8	/v/	as in	very	/ˈvɛri/
9	/s/	as in	son	/sʌn/
10	/z/	as in	zoo	/zu/
11	/l/	as in	live	/lɪv/
12	/m/	as in	my	/maɪ/
13	/n/	as in	near	/nɪr/
14	/h/	as in	happy	/ˈhæpi/
15	/r/	as in	red	/rɛd/
16	/y/	as in	yes	/yɛs/
17	/w/	as in	want	/wɑnt/
18	/θ/	as in	thanks	/θæŋks/
19	/ð/	as in	the	/ðə/
20	/ʃ/	as in	she	/ʃi/
21	/ʒ/	as in	television	/ˈtɛləvɪʒn/
22	/tʃ/	as in	child	/tʃaɪld/
23	/dʒ/	as in	Japan	/dʒəˈpæn/
24	/ŋ/	as in	English	/ˈɪŋglɪʃ/

Vowels

25	/i/	as in	see	/si/
26	/ɪ/	as in	his	/hɪz/
27	/ɛ/	as in	ten	/tɛn/
28	/æ/	as in	stamp	/stæmp/
29	/ɑ/	as in	father	/ˈfɑðər/
30	/ɔ/	as in	saw	/sɔ/
31	/ɒ/	as in	hot	/hɒt/
32	/ʊ/	as in	book	/bʊk/
33	/u/	as in	you	/yu/
34	/ʌ/	as in	sun	/sʌn/
35	/ə/	as in	about	/əˈbaʊt/
36	/eɪ/	as in	name	/neɪm/
37	/aɪ/	as in	my	/maɪ/
38	/ɔɪ/	as in	boy	/bɔɪ/
39	/aʊ/	as in	how	/haʊ/
40	/oʊ/	as in	go	/goʊ/
41	/ər/	as in	bird	/bərd/
42	/ɪr/	as in	near	/nɪr/
43	/ɛr/	as in	hair	/hɛr/
44	/ɑr/	as in	car	/kɑr/
45	/ɔr/	as in	more	/mɔr/
46	/ʊr/	as in	tour	/tʊr/

OXFORD
UNIVERSITY PRESS

Great Clarendon Street, Oxford, OX2 6DP, United Kingdom

Oxford University Press is a department of the University of Oxford.
It furthers the University's objective of excellence in research, scholarship,
and education by publishing worldwide. Oxford is a registered trade
mark of Oxford University Press in the UK and in certain other countries

© Oxford University Press 2011

The moral rights of the author have been asserted

First published in 2011

2015 2014 2013 2012 2011

10 9 8 7 6 5 4 3 2 1

No unauthorized photocopying

All rights reserved. No part of this publication may be reproduced, stored in a retrieval system, or transmitted, in any form or by any means, without the prior permission in writing of Oxford University Press, or as expressly permitted by law, by licence or under terms agreed with the appropriate reprographics rights organization. Enquiries concerning reproduction outside the scope of the above should be sent to the ELT Rights Department, Oxford University Press, at the address above

You must not circulate this work in any other form and you must impose this same condition on any acquirer

Links to third party websites are provided by Oxford in good faith and for information only. Oxford disclaims any responsibility for the materials contained in any third party website referenced in this work

ISBN: 978 0 19 472777 8   Student book with Multi-ROM Pack
ISBN: 978 0 19 472756 3   Student book
ISBN: 978 0 19 472768 6   Multi-ROM pack

Printed in China

This book is printed on paper from certified and well-managed sources

ACKNOWLEDGEMENTS

The authors and publisher are grateful to those who have given permission to reproduce the following extracts and adaptations of copyright materials: p.10 'Welcome to Our World: The Qus: Beijing, China'; *The Guardian*, 21st October 2006. Copyright Guardian News and Media Ltd 2006; p.11 'Welcome to Our World: The Kamaus Ongata Rongai, Kenya'; *The Guardian*, 21st October 2006. Reproduced by kind permission of Xan Rice; p.12 'A world in one family': interviews reproduced with kind permission of Ana Reynoso and family; pp.19–20 Adapted extracts from 'The Best of Times'; *Majesty Magazine*, November 2006. Reproduced by kind permission of Majesty Magazine; p.24 'Smash! Museum visitor trips on lace and destroys priceless vases'; *The Daily Telegraph*, 30th January 2006. Copyright The Telegraph Media Group Ltd; pp.26–7 Extracts from 'Romeo and Juliet', Oxford World Classics; © Oxford University Press 2000; pp.33 'I Believe' Words and Music by Ian Dury and Michael Gallagher © Templemill Music and Mute Song. All rights reserved on behalf of Templemill Music administered by Warner/Chappell Music Ltd, London W6 8BS. Reproduced by permission; p.35 'You don't know you are born', *The Sunday Times*, 11th February 2007 © NI Syndication, London (2007) p.41 'Rocket Man, Steve Bennett'; BBC-Saturday Live, 10/03/2007. © BBC Radio. Reproduced with kind permission of Steve Bennett, Starchaser Plc and BBC Radio. pp.42–3 'Year 2025: We'll find aliens, talk to animals and be sprightly at 100'; from *Daily Mail*, 16/11/2006 © Daily Mail 2006.

Although every effort has been made to trace and contact copyright holders before publication, this has not been possible in some cases. We apologize for any apparent infringement of copyright and if notified, the publisher will be pleased to rectify any errors or omissions at the earliest opportunity.

Illustrations by: Tim Branch: p.24 (yin yang); Gill Button: pp.21, 32, 40; Melvyn Evans: p.37 (rocket); Leo Hartas: p.101; Detmeer Otto: pp.2, 3; Gavin Reece: pp.12, 22-23, 104, 144.

Commissioned photography by: Gareth Boden: pp.5, 10 (Jenny & Mike), p.143; Paul Freestone: p.8 (Ana Reynoso and family); Mark Mason: pp.81.

We would also like to thank the following for permission to reproduce the following photographs: Alamy Images: p.5 (dog/Jeremy Pardoe); p.5 (saxophone/i love images); p.9 (Jupiterimages/Creatas); p.10 (Vicky/Travelshots.com); p.16 (cooking/A Room with Views); p.16 (gym/Buzz Pictures); p.16 (tennis/moodboard); p.16 (music/the box studio); p.16 (cycling/Ingram Publishing/Superstock Limited); p.34 (rainforest/Ern Mainka); p.37 (Space Shuttle Discovery/KPA/Galaxy/Content Mine International); p.44 (Mamma Mia jar/Martin Lee/Mediablitzimages (UK) Ltd); p.45 (Devon cottage/Elizabeth Whiting & Associates); p.45 (watch/Synthetic Alan King); p.49 (shoppers/Ian Dagnall); (Billy small photo); Steve Baxter: p.20 (fallen visitor); Mahesh Bhat: p.47 (Lakshmamma); The Bridgeman Art Library: p.18 (Vincent van Gogh, Self Portrait, 1889, Private Collection); p.18 (Vincent van Gogh, Irises, 1889, Private Collection); p.18 (Vincent van Gogh, Red Vineyards at Arles, 1888, Pushkin Museum, Moscow); p.19 (Vincent van Gogh, Sunflowers, 1888. Neue Pinakothek, Munich, Germany); p.50; Camera Press: p. 14 (H.R.H. Prince Charles/Photography by Ian Jones/Gamma); p. 15 (H.R.H. Prince Charles and H.R.H. Camilla, Duchess of Cornwall/Richard Gillard); Casio Electronics Company Limited: p. 30 (Casio EXLIM Zoom EX-Z9 digital compact camera); Christie's Images: p.59 (old football boots and football); Corbis: p.9 (canoeing/David Madison); p.39 (polar bears/epa); p.37 (Jules Verne rocket, From the Earth to the Moon, 1872/Bettmann); p.45 (father and son/Alexander Scott/

zefa); p.102 (Mother Teresa smiling/Reuters); p. 102 (Mother Teresa serious/JP Laffont/Sygma); Creative Technology Ltd: p.30 (Creative Zen Vision MP3 Player); Dorling Kindersley: p. 45 (Teddy bear); Reproduction by permission of the Syndics of the Fitzwilliam Museum, Cambridge: p.20 (Chinese porcelain vases c. 1680–1720); Getty Images: p.14 (Dave/Peter Dazeley/The Image Bank); p.15 (Sean Davey); p.18 (The Royal Family on the balcony/Daniel Berehulak); p.15 (Prince Charles with Princes William and Harry/Tim Graham Photo Library); p.16 (LWA/Photodisc); p.25 (John Cumming/Iconica); p.26 (questions/Jed Share/Photographer's Choice); p.29 (Millie/Photographer's Choice); p.29 (Frank/Marc Romanelli/Photographer's Choice); p.39 (galaxy/Ian Mckinnell/Photographer's Choice); p.46 (tarts/Heidi Coppock-Beard/Stone); p.47 (Elizabeth Anne Hogan/Stephanie Diani); p.48 (Grant Faint/The Image Bank); p.49 (coffee/Sergio Pitamitz/Iconica); p.49 (escalator with couple/Justin Pumfrey/Iconica); p.143 (introducing/Somos/Veer); p.143 (hotel room/Johannes Kroemer); p.143 (dinner party); Courtesy of Gibson Guitars: p.45 (ES335 guitar); Grazia Neri: p.47 (Santina Corvaglia/Franco Origlia); p.102 (young Mother Teresa/Giovanbattista Brambilla); iStockphoto: p.5 (paperclip and page/Christoph Weihs); p.5 (laptop/muharrem öner) p.9, 16 (painting/Thye Aun Ngo); p.16 (gardening/Alex Hinds); p.16 (photography/blackred); p.26 (mannequin and question/Palto); p.27 (two mannequins/emmgunn); p.27 (sign post/Vasiliy Yakobchuk); p.28 (paper/Clayton Hansen); p.28 (lined paper/Bruce Lonngren); p.47 (camera/fajean); p.47 (laptop/shapecharge); p.48 (Kos boat/Alfred Rijnders); p.48 (newspaper ad/Bruce Lonngren); p.44 (Mamma Mia illustration); p.45 (pills/Bill Fehr); p.46 (tablecloth); christine balderas); p.96 (paper/Trevor Hunt); p.96 (paper/Christopher Hudson); Dave King: p.31 (The Gregory family); MTV Networks UK & Ireland: p.30 (robot I Sobot Robot); Masterfile: p.41 (Pierre Tremblay); Ben McMillan: p.7 (The Qus family); National Motor Museum: p.31 (camper van); Nixon: p.30 (Nixon bag); PA Photos: p.37 (Steve Bennett/Owen Humphreys/PA Archive); Panos Pictures: p.6 (The Kamaus family/Sven Torfin); Philips: p. 30 (Philips widescreen TV); p.30 (Philips DC200 IPOD dock); Punchstock: p.7 (map/BLOOMimage); p.10 (Terry/image100); p.13 (Stockbyte); p.16 (camping/Radius Images); p.17 (Stockbyte); p.29 (Richard/Anthony-Masterson/Digital Vision); p.34 (BLOOMimage); p.34 (gorilla/Gerry Ellis/Digital Vision); p.34 (ice and snow/Eastcott Momatiuk/Digital Vision); p.39 (running/Colin Anderson/Blend Images); p.39 (Chad Baker/Digital Vision); p.29 (Ian Dury/Brian Rasic); p.51 (three fans reading/James Fraser); Anna Rianne: p.32 (sign); p.40 (NOAA); p.41 (Apollo 11/NASA); Seiko Europe Limited: p.30 (Orange Monster Watch); Sony Computer Entertainment Europe: p.30 (Playstation 3); Sony Ericsson UK & Ireland: p.30 (Sony Ericsson W910i mobile phone); Sony UK Limited: p.30 (Sony Vaio notebook computer); Tomy Corporation: p.30 (Rock Band Guitar (based on a Fender Stratocaster used for Rock Band computer game published by MTV Games WeSC - WeAretheSuperlativeConspiracy: p.30 (headphones); www.all-the-flags-of-the-world.c.la: p.8 (Bolivia); (Union Jack); (Basque); BAA Aviation Photolibrary, www.baa.com/photolibrary: p.143 (airport information); Tetra Images/Alamy: p. 4 Photographer's Choice/Getty Images: Murat Taner: p.5 (Empire State Building); Graphi-Ogre/oup: p.8 (Peruvian and American flags); Goodshoot/Jupiterimages/AGE Fotostock: p.10 (waiter); Stockbyte/Alamy: George Doyle p.10 (policeman); Photodisc/Oxford University Press: pp.13, 143 (money); Asia Pac/Getty Images: Pool p.15 (Prince Charles in Asia); Fancy Collection/Superstock: p.16 (shopping); Radius/Superstock: p.17 (Chicago); Brand X Pictures/Jupiter Images: Jack Hollingsworth p.24 (woman); Jupiter Images: Jose Luis Pelaez Inc.: p.24 (boy); Masterfile: Kevin Dodge: p.24 (man); Jupiter Images/Brand X/Alamy: p.28 (Creatas Images/AGE Fotostock: p.34 (man and woman reading a newspaper); Alamy: Frantisek Staud: p.34 (indegenous people); Reuters: Manuel Silvestri: p.34 (Venice piazza flooded); Photographer's Choice/Getty Images: Georgette Douwma: p.34 (underwater life); mauritius images/AGE Fotostock: Peter von Felber: p.42 ; AGE Fotostock/Johnny Stockshooter: p.99 (Philadelphia Museum of Art).